I am thankful to the universe for all its blessings, and I hold the belief that the essence of existence lies in bringing meaning to the lives of others.
Good painting!

Alex Eliot
2024

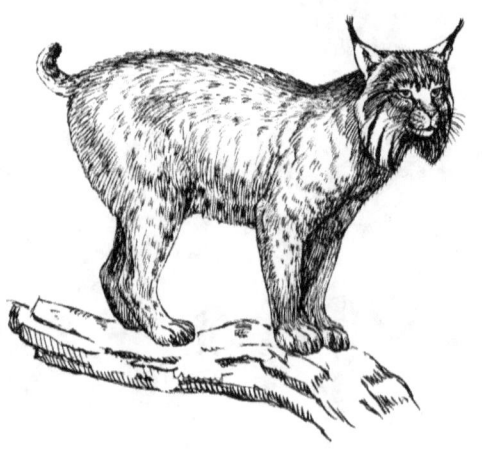
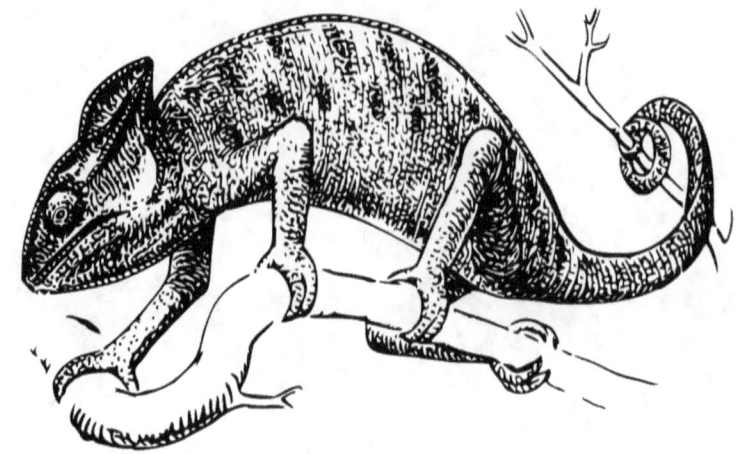

This Book Belongs to:

―――――――――――――――――――

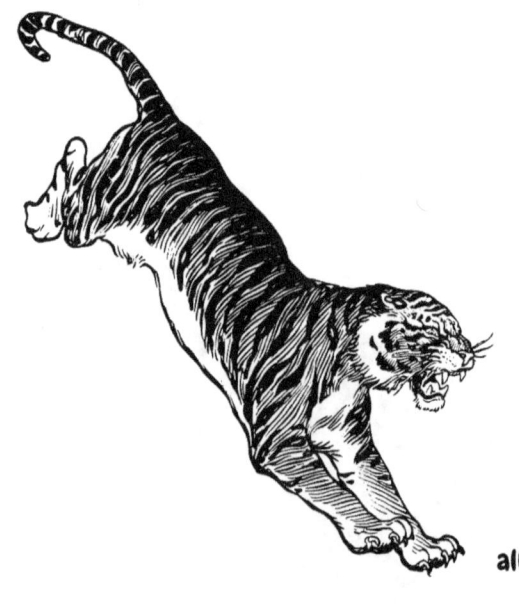
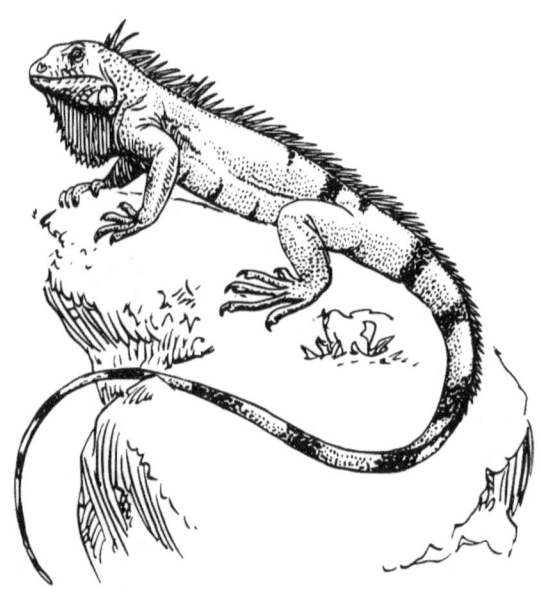

A.E.B©
all rights reserved

ALL RIGHTS RESERVED©
2024

No part of this publication may be reproduced, distributed, or transmitted in any form or by any means, including photocopying, recording, or other electronic or mechanical methods, without the prior written permission of the publisher, except for brief quotations incorporated in critical reviews and other specific noncommercial uses. Any unauthorized replica of this work is prohibited.

A.E.B©
Alex's Eliot Books

Test Color Page

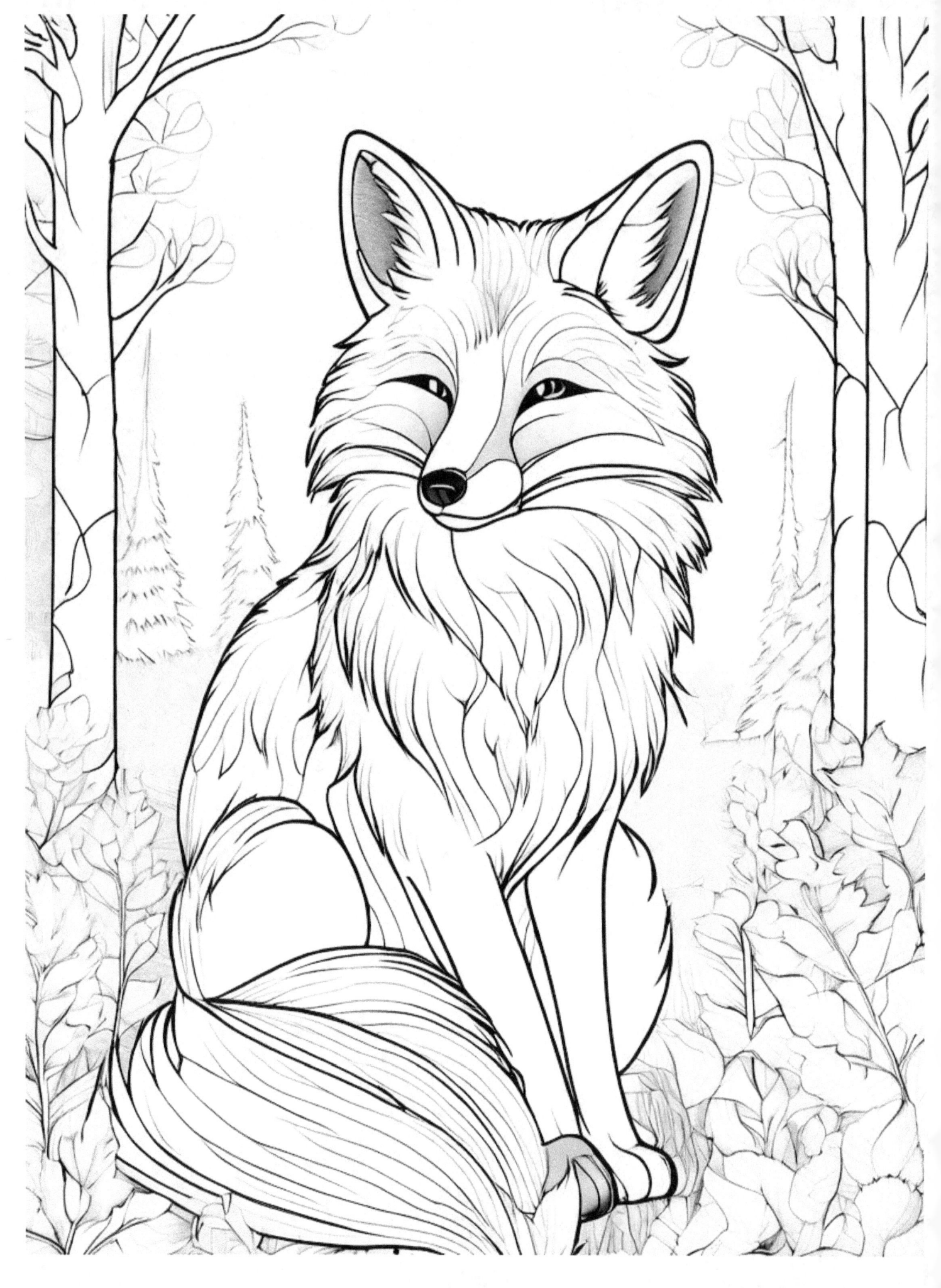

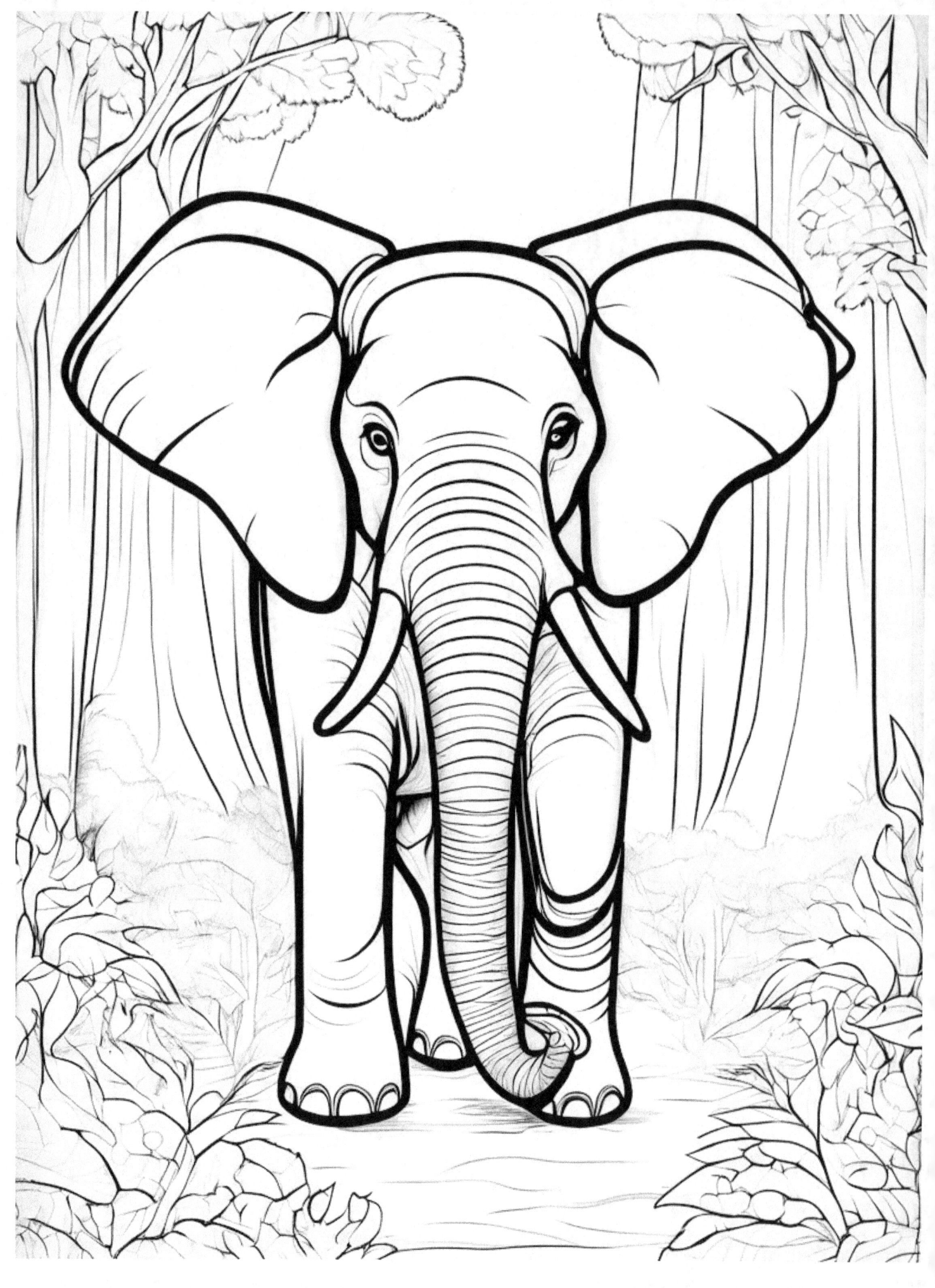

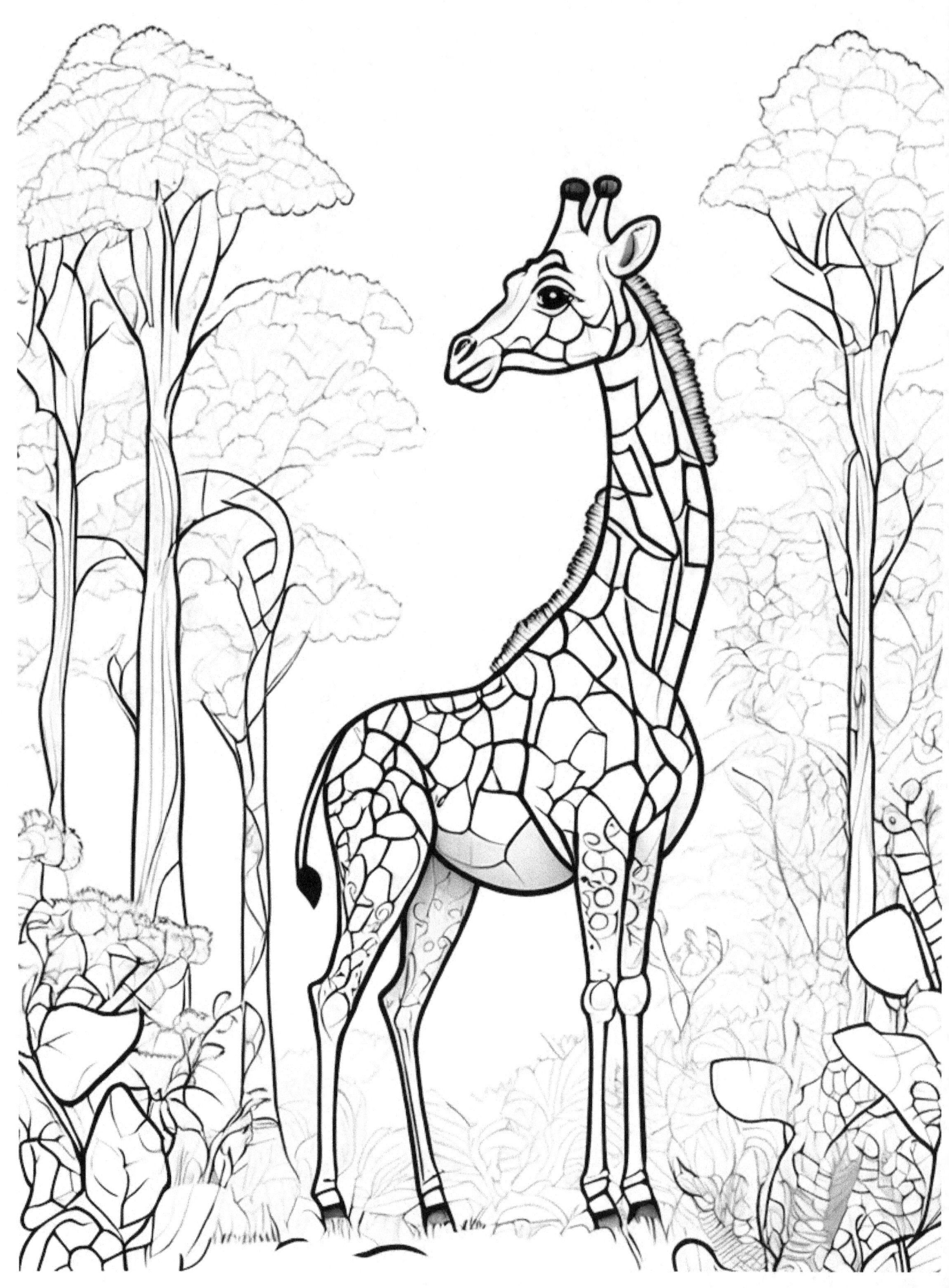

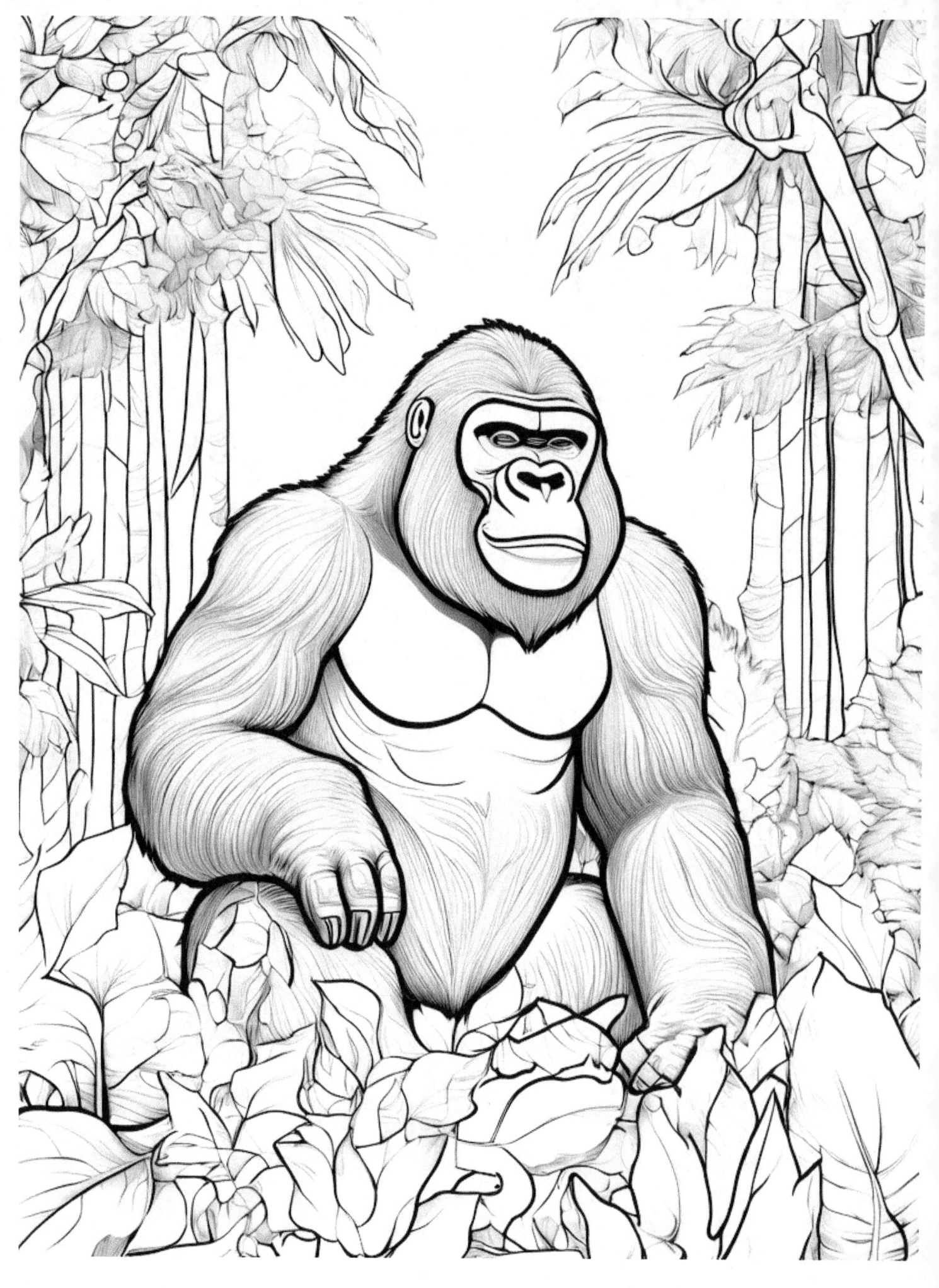

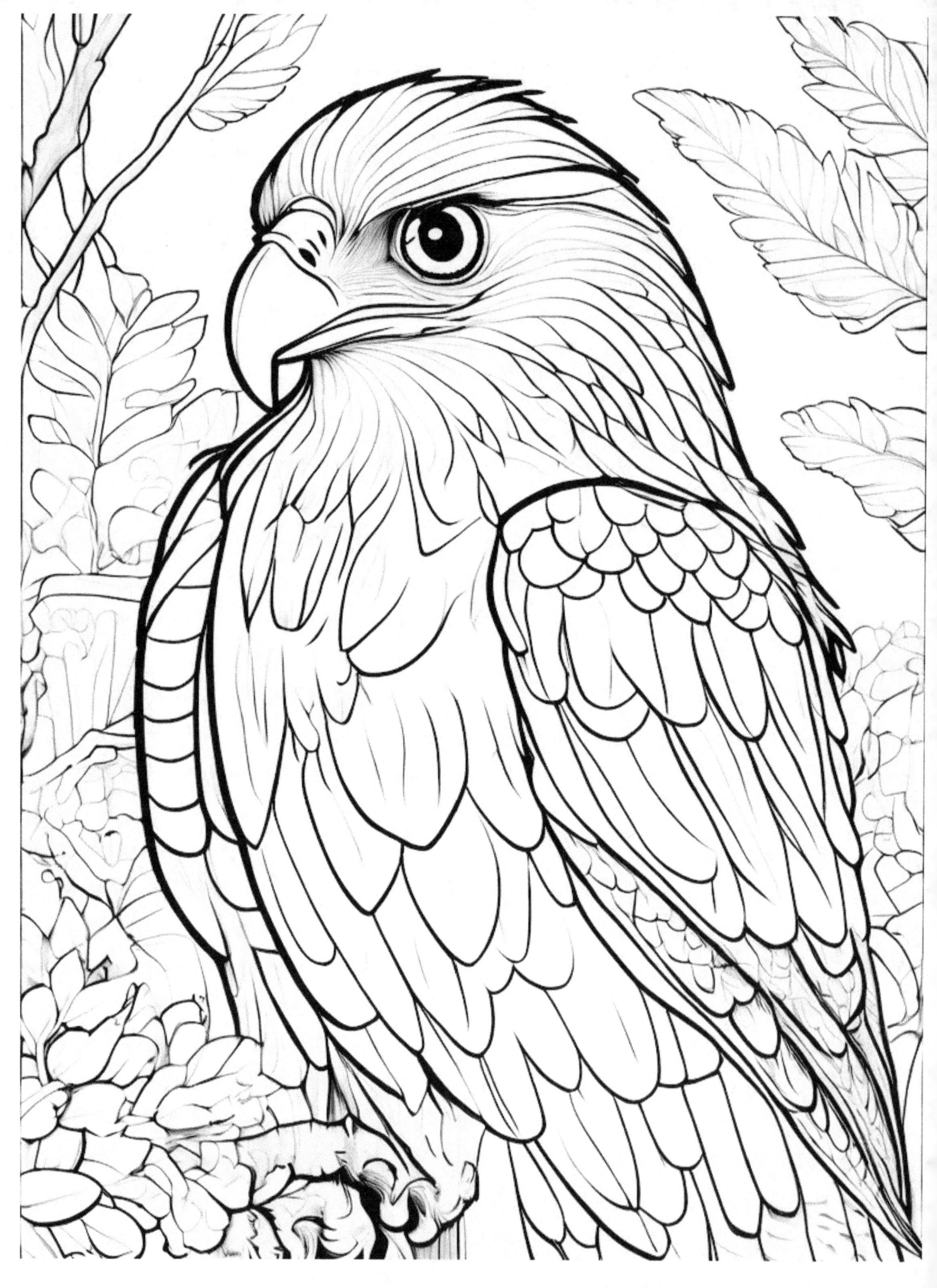

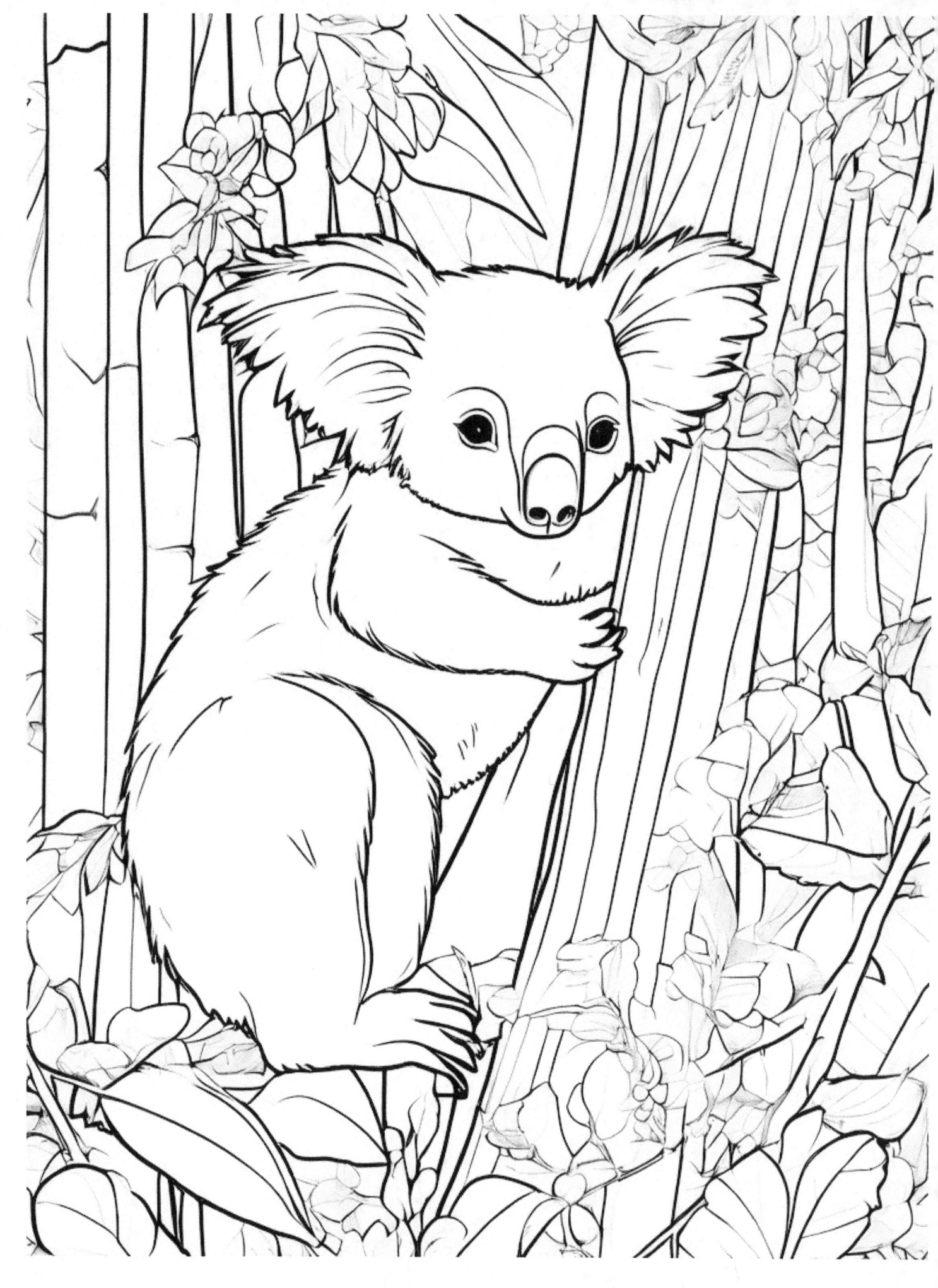

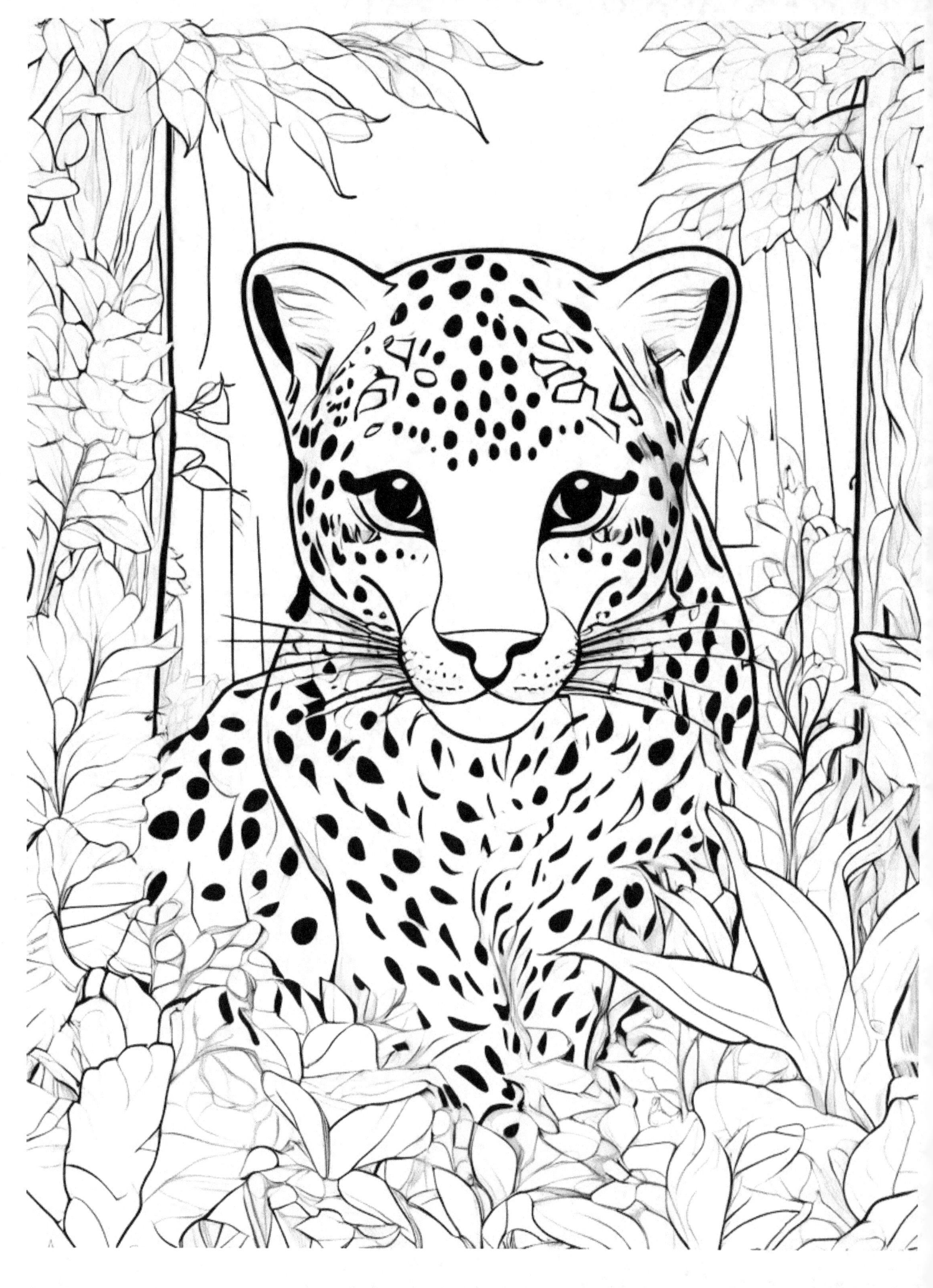

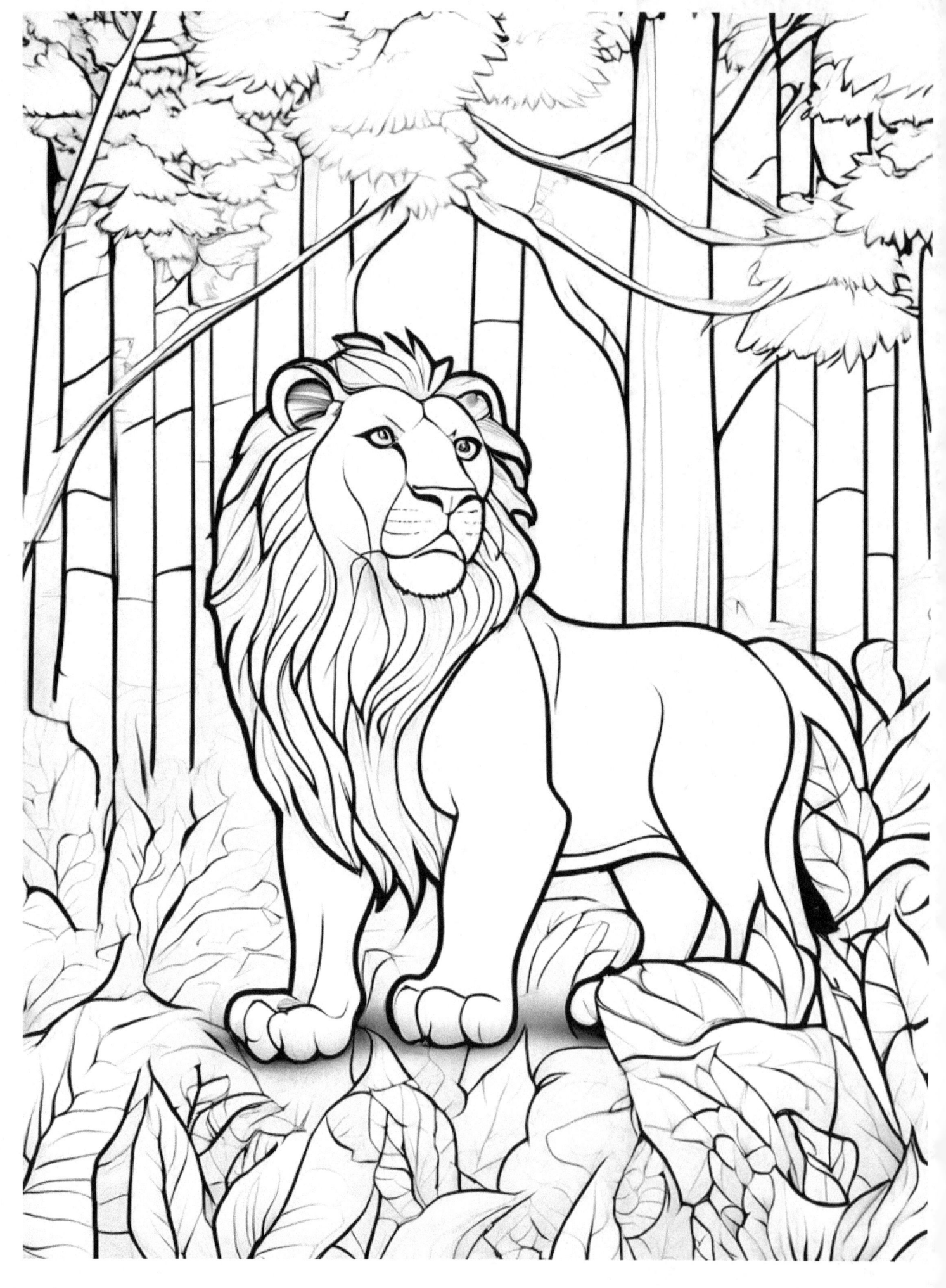

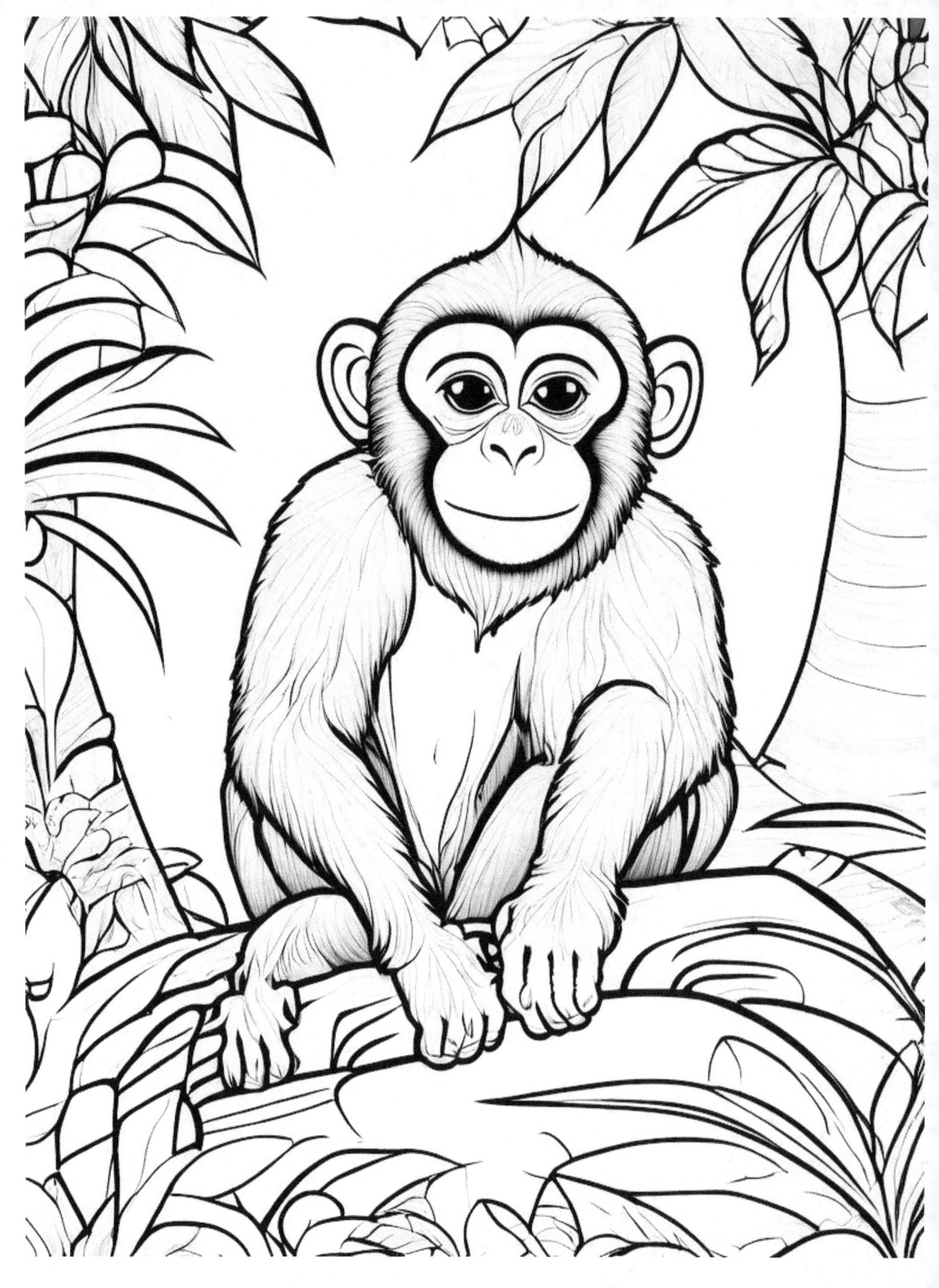

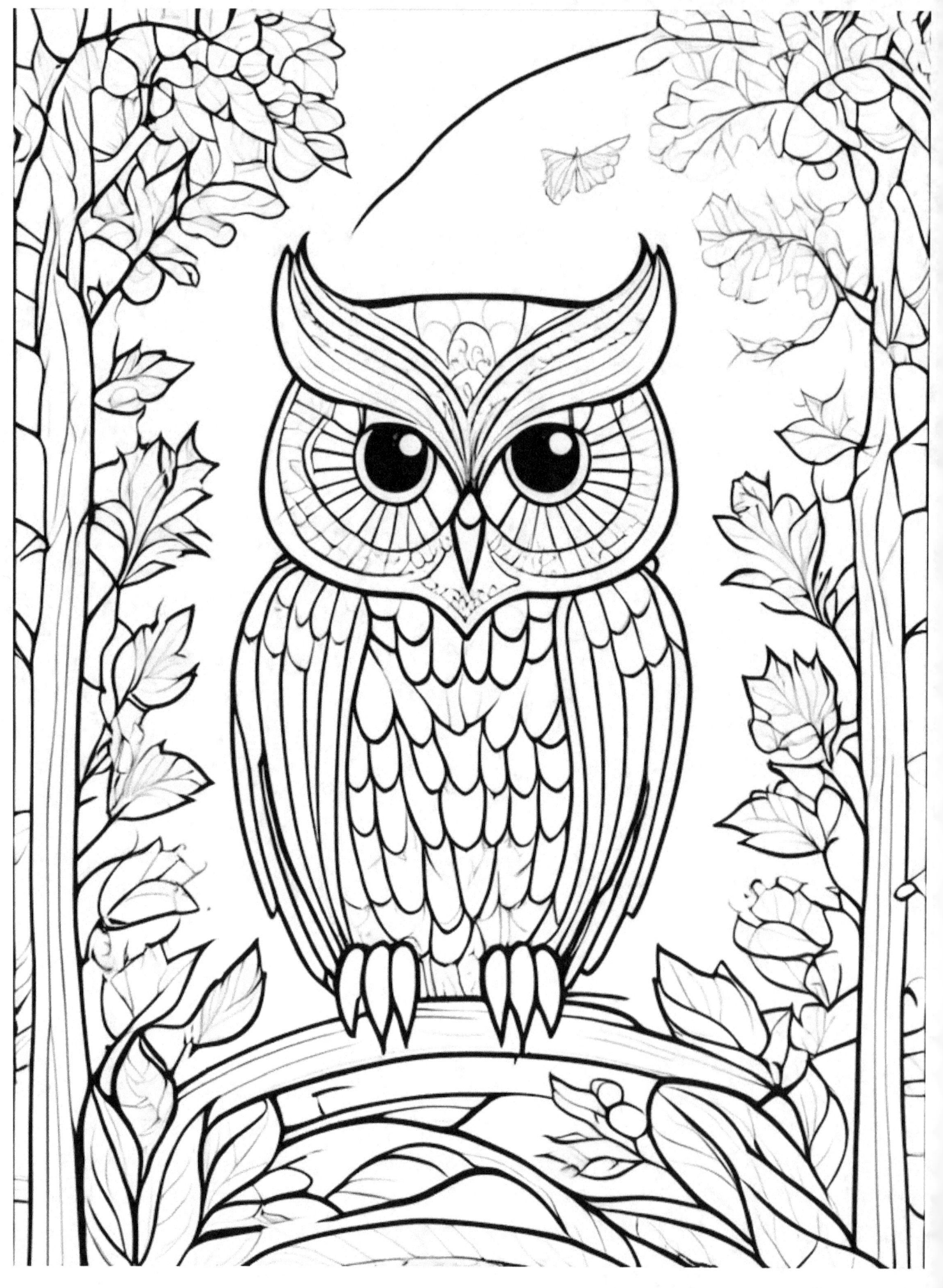

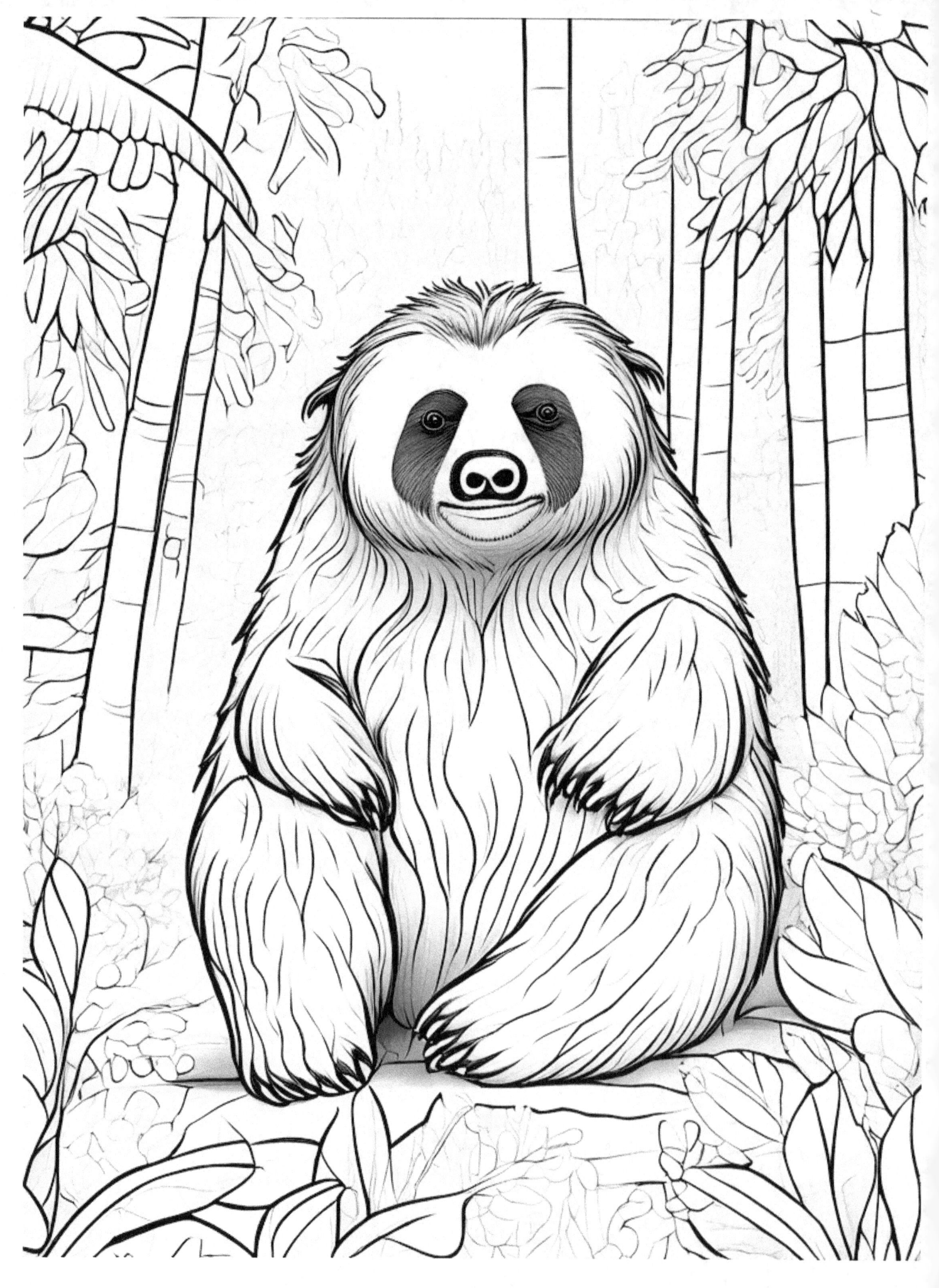

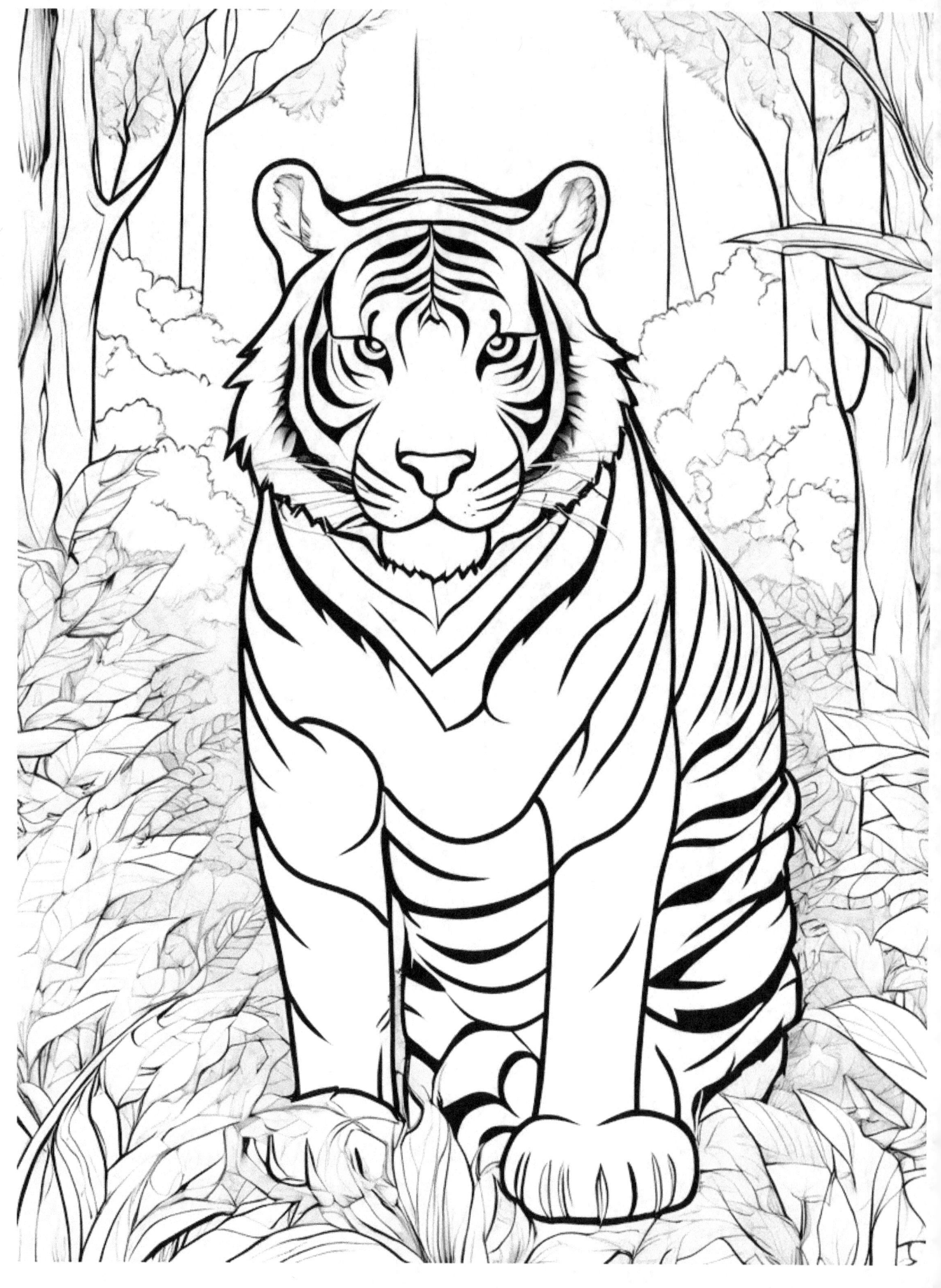

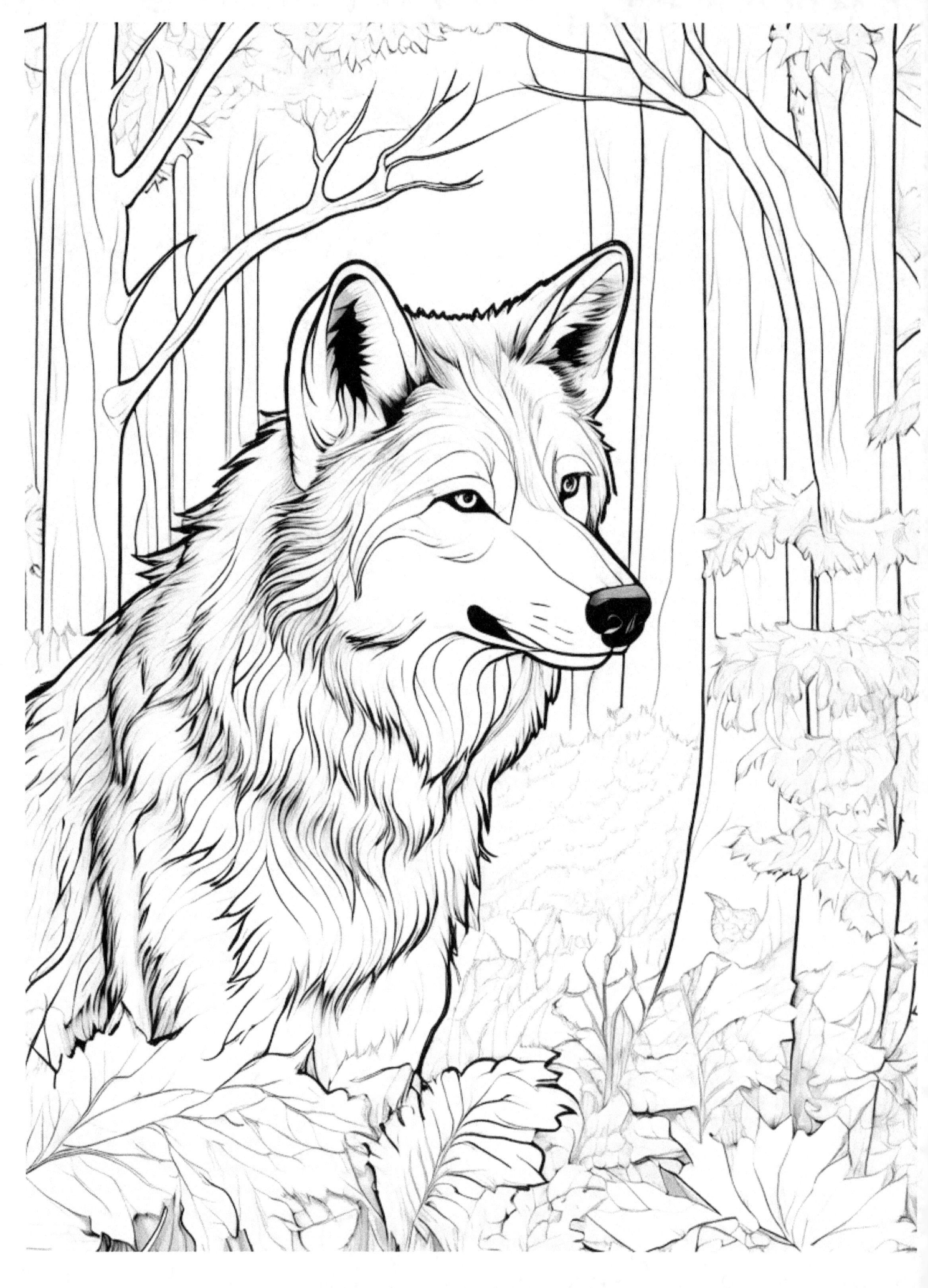

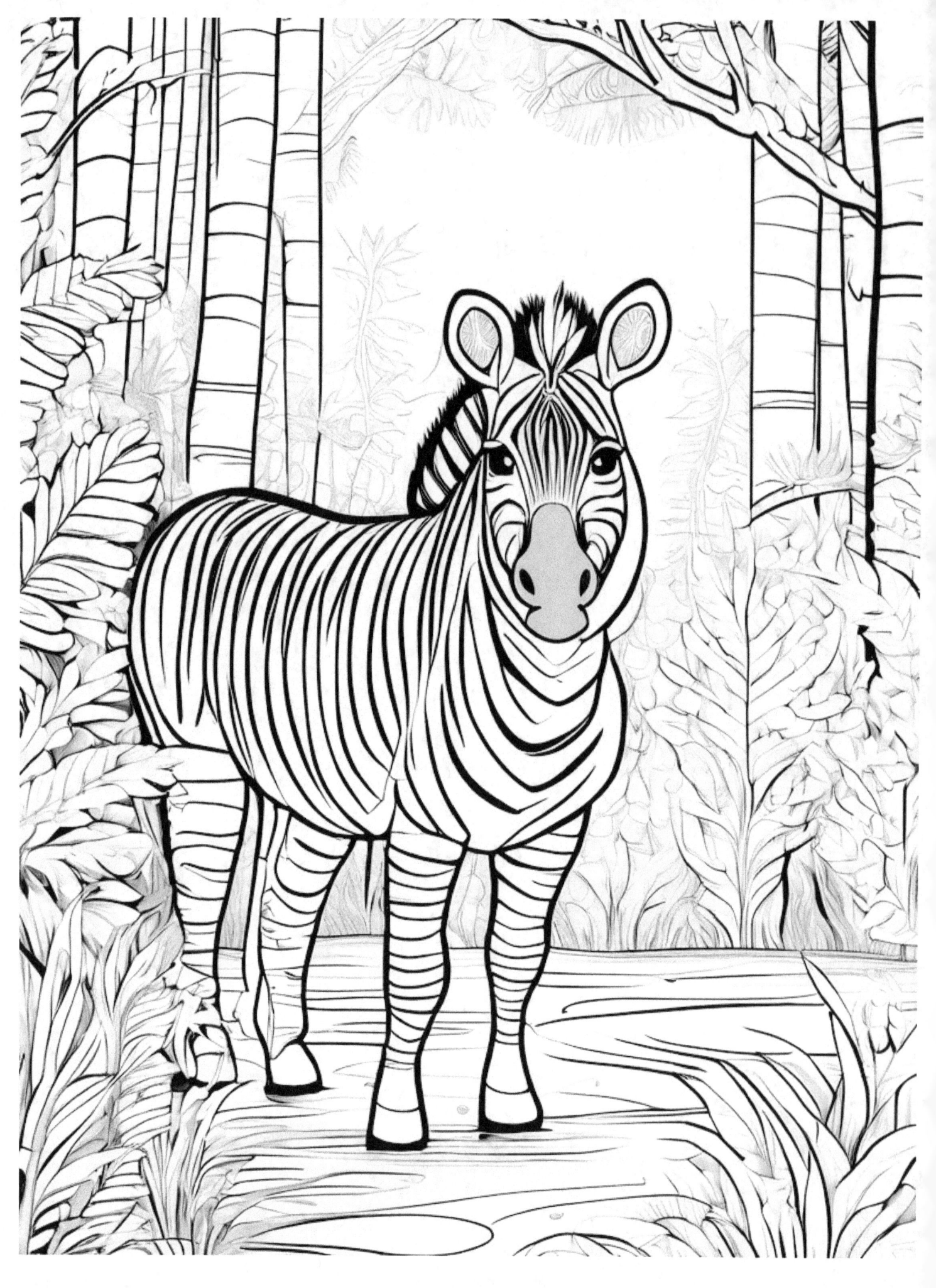

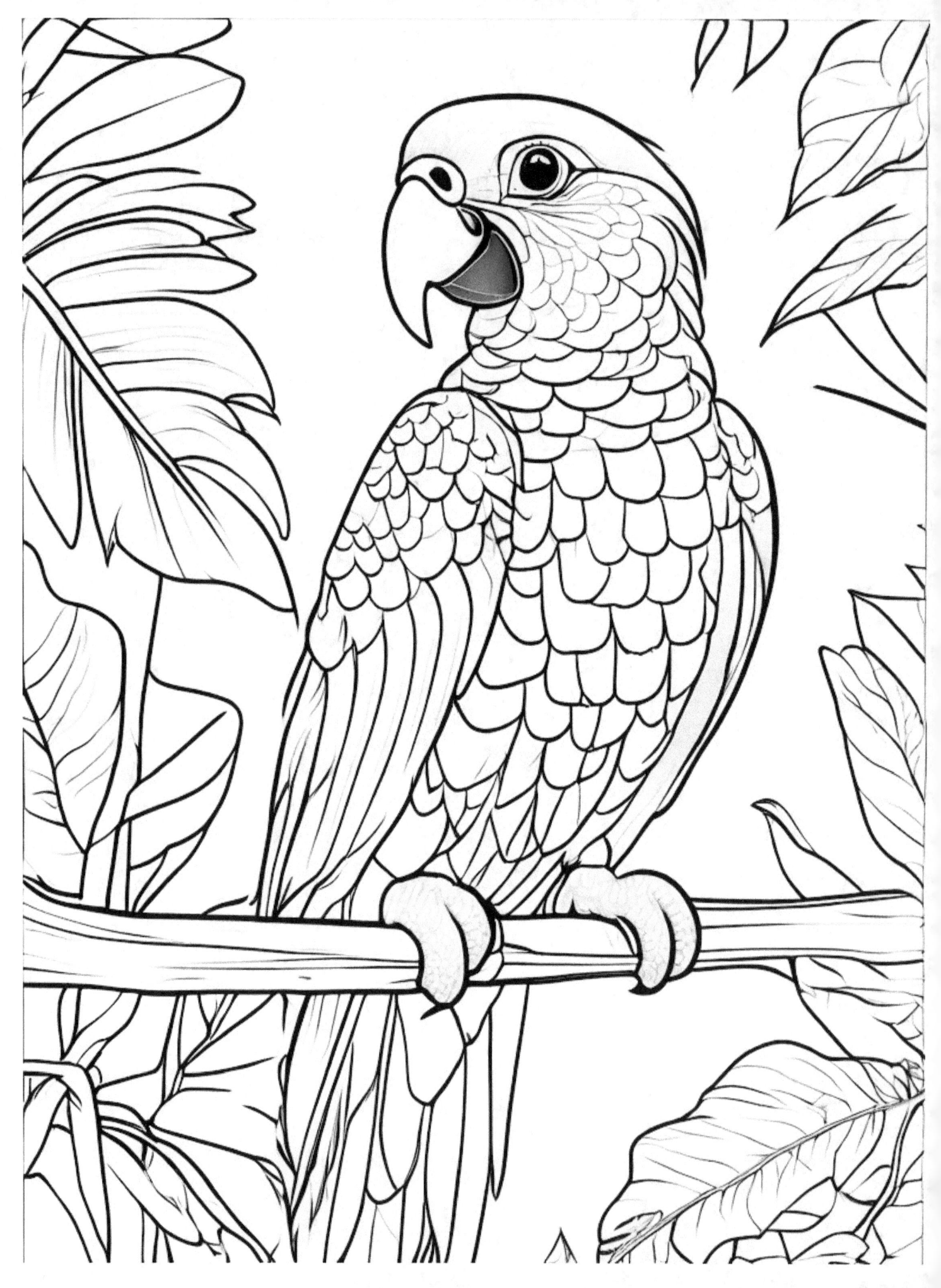

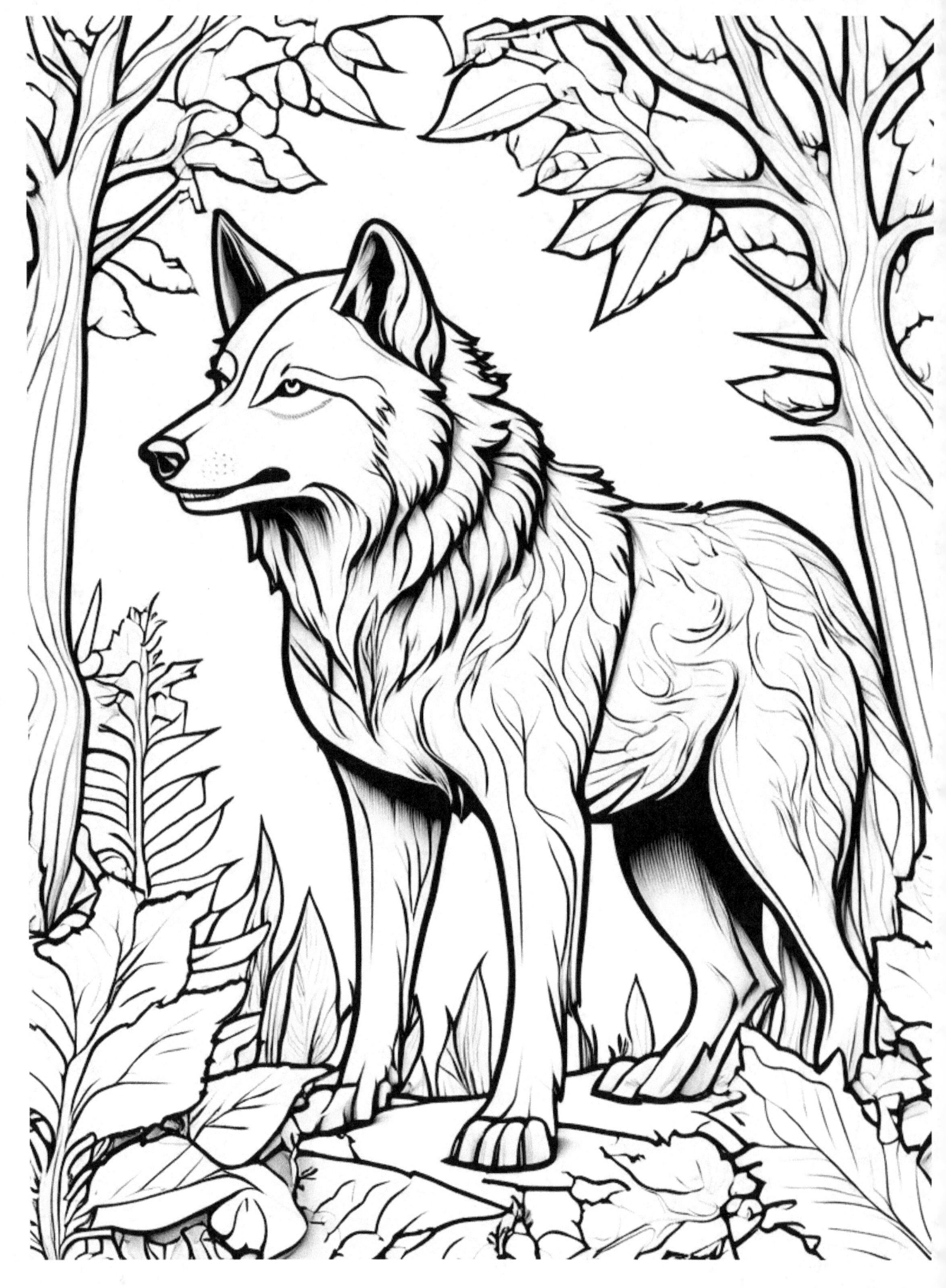

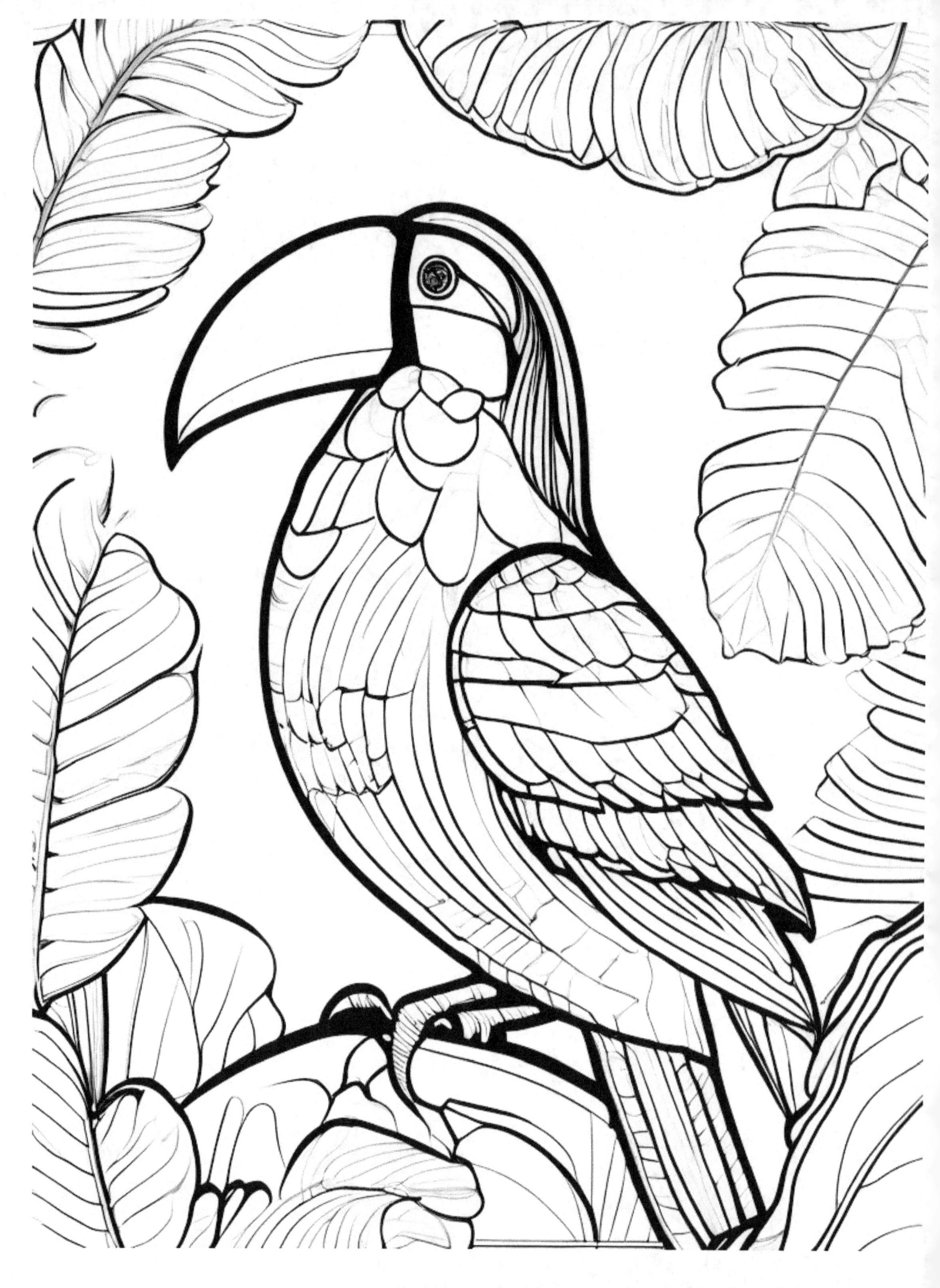

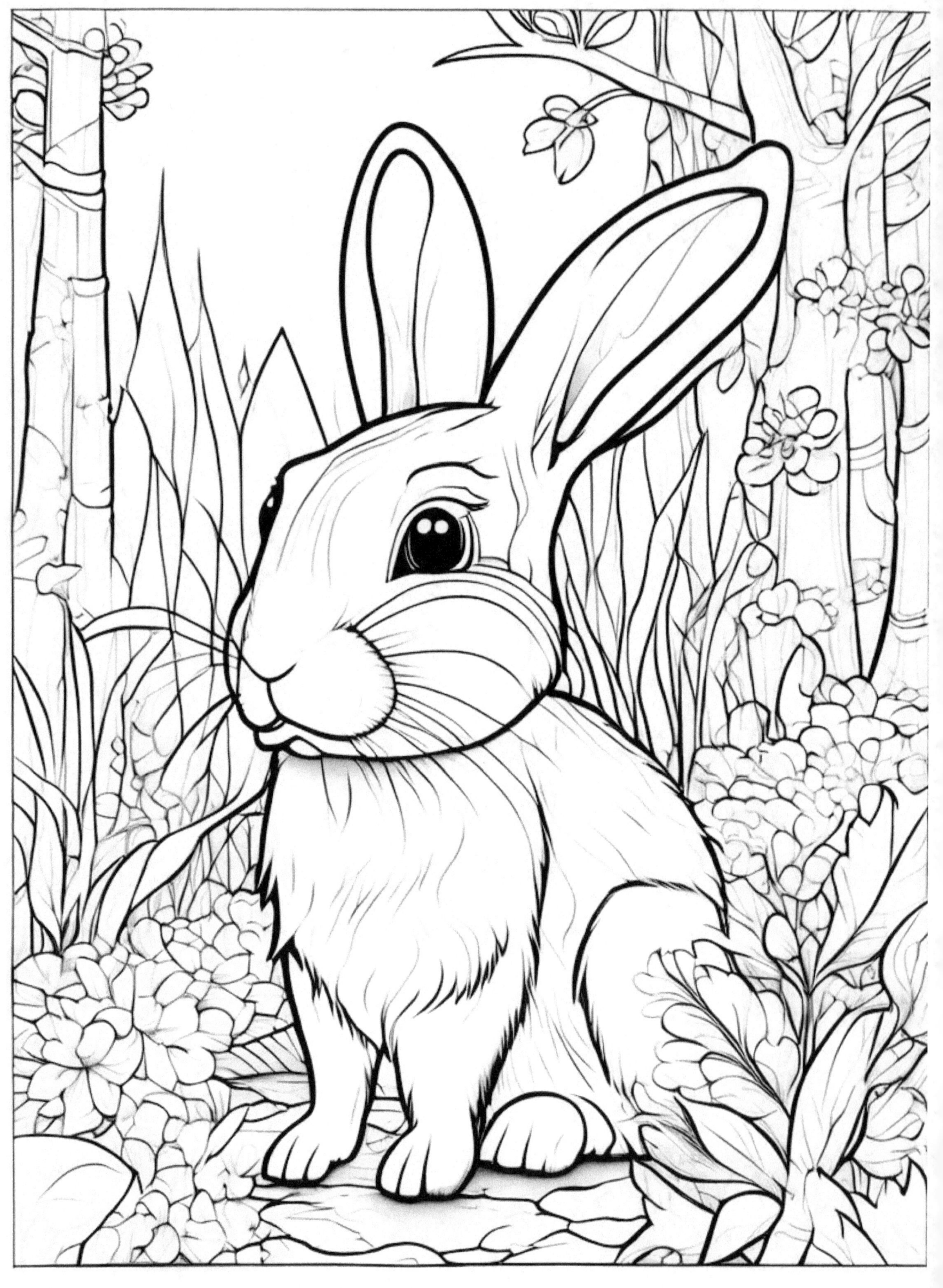

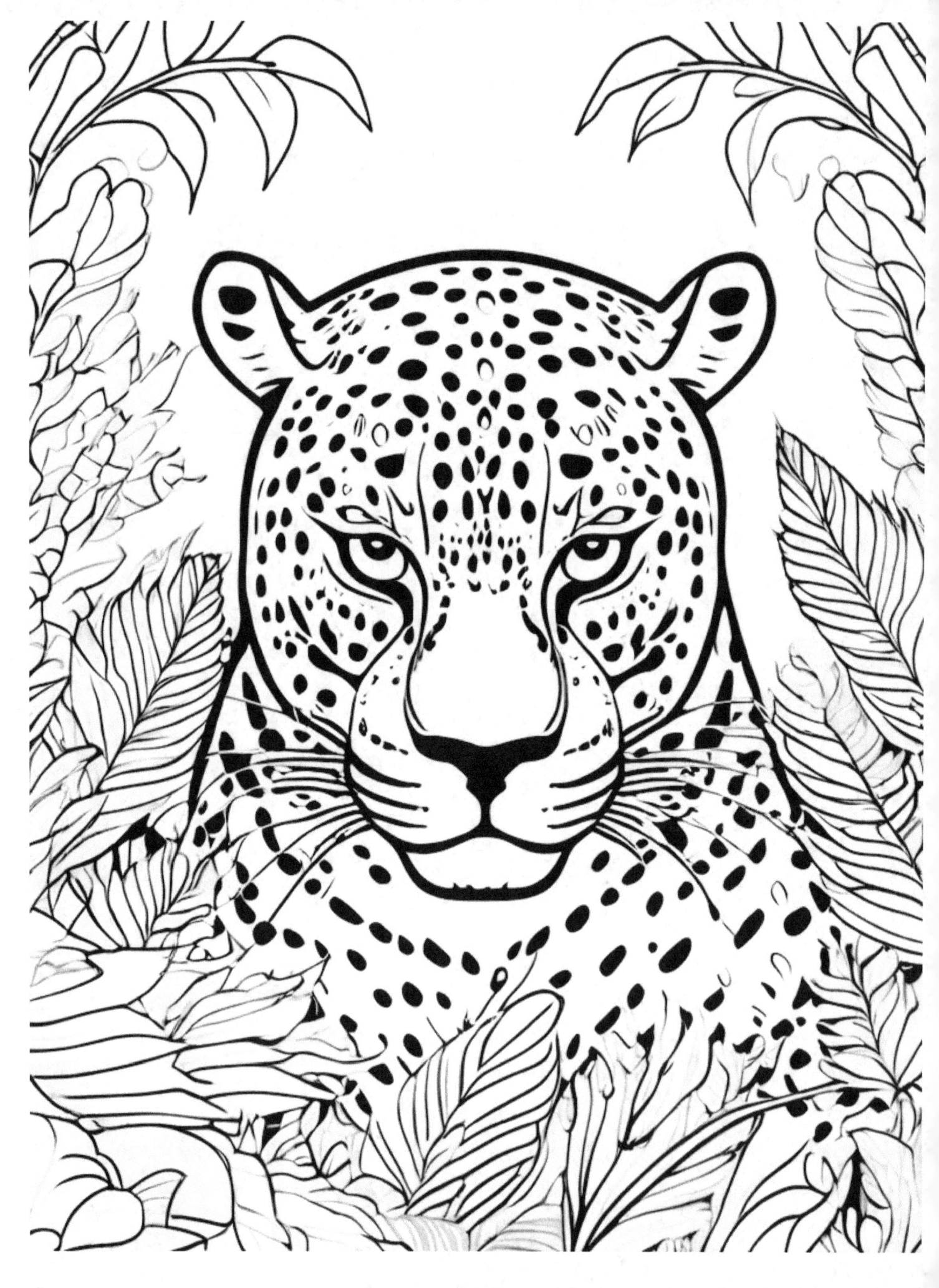

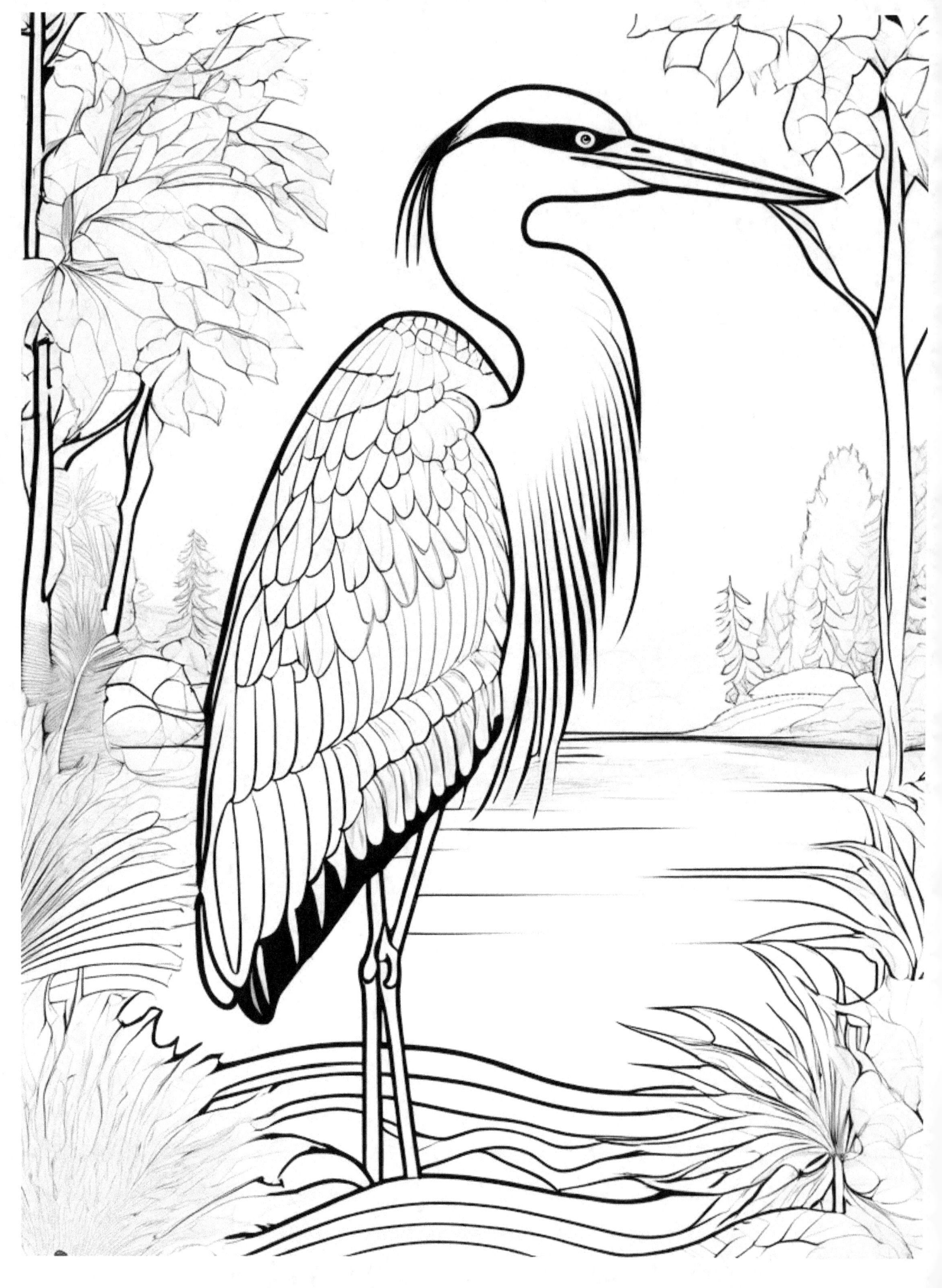

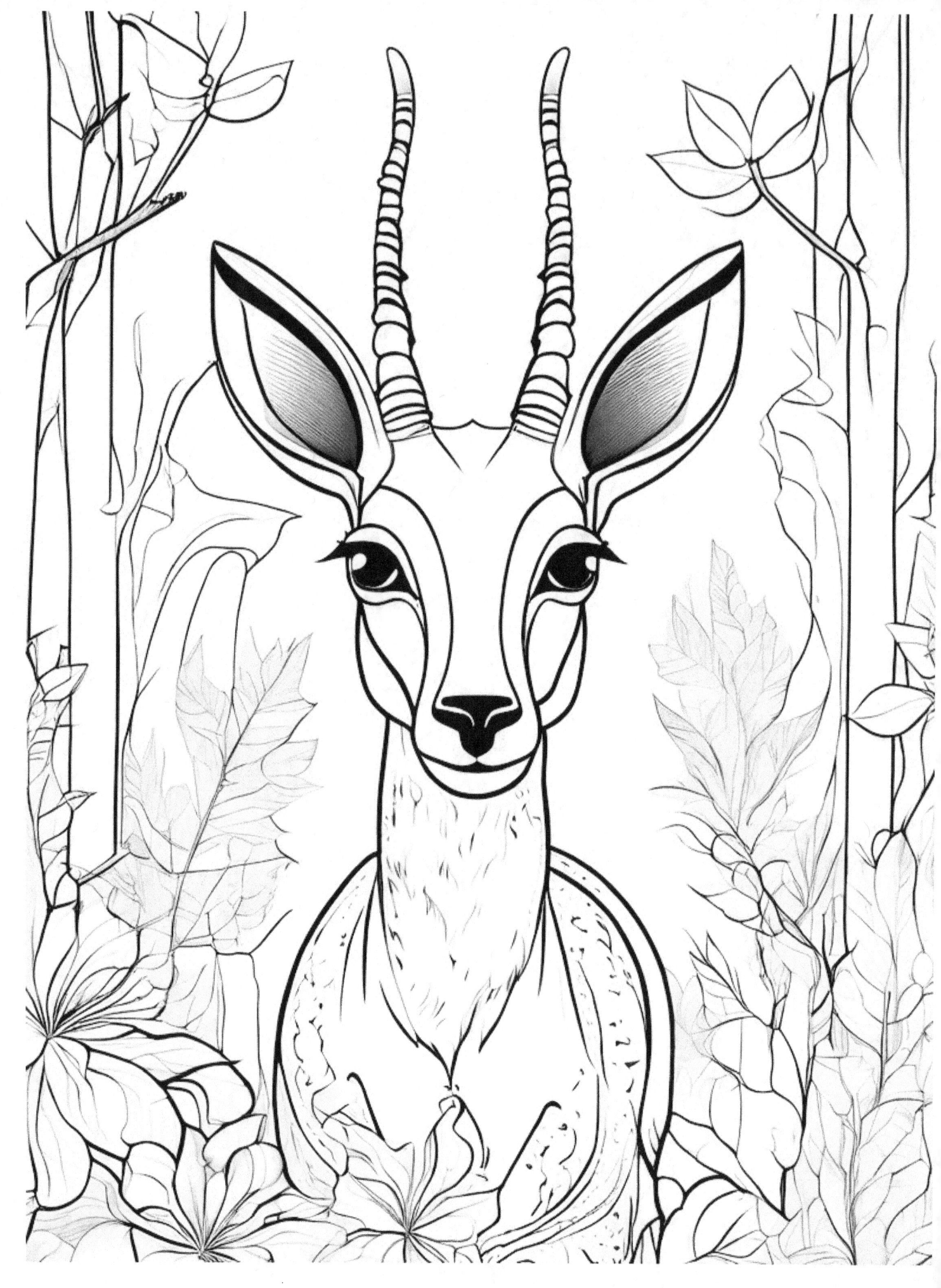

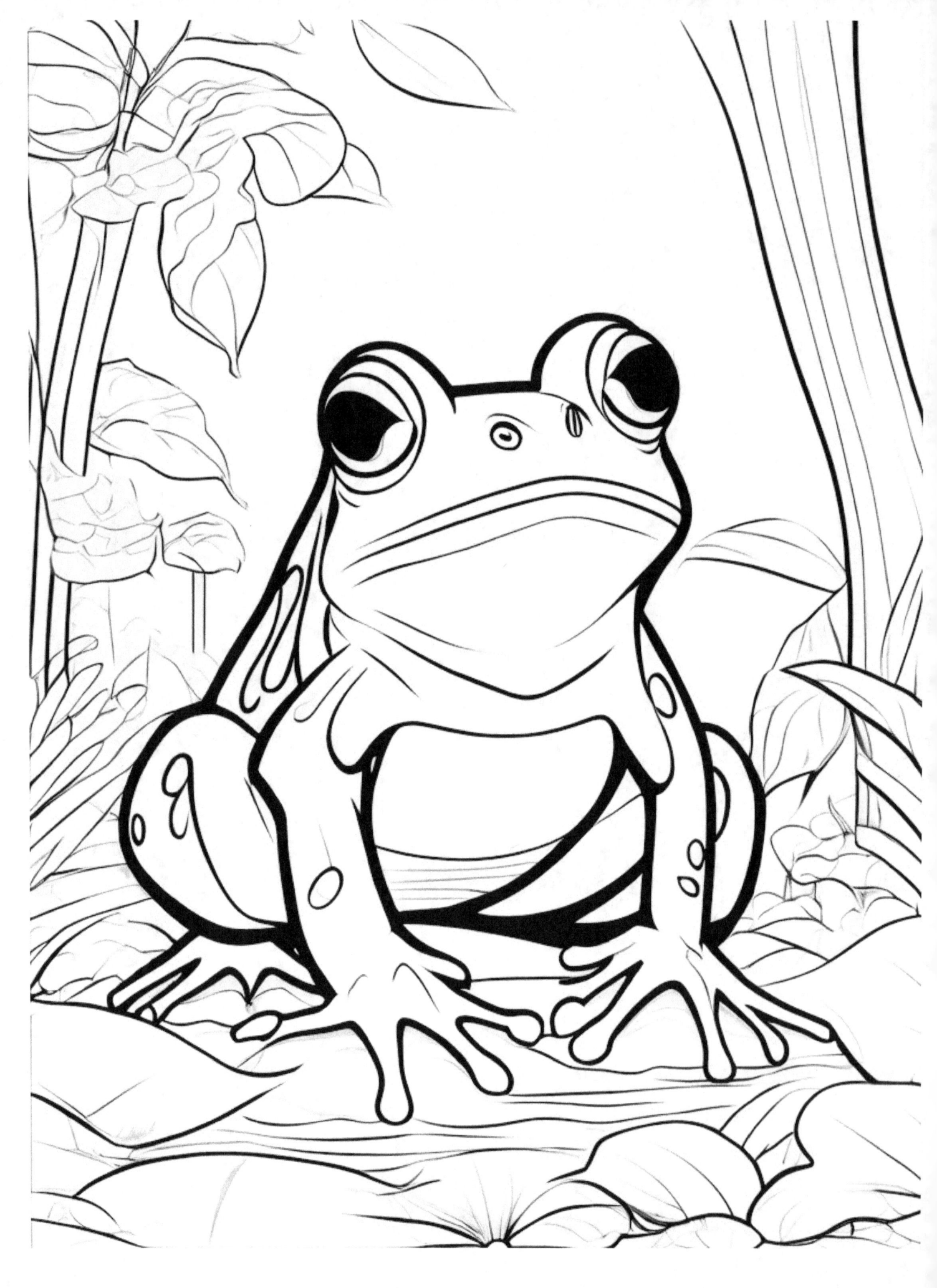

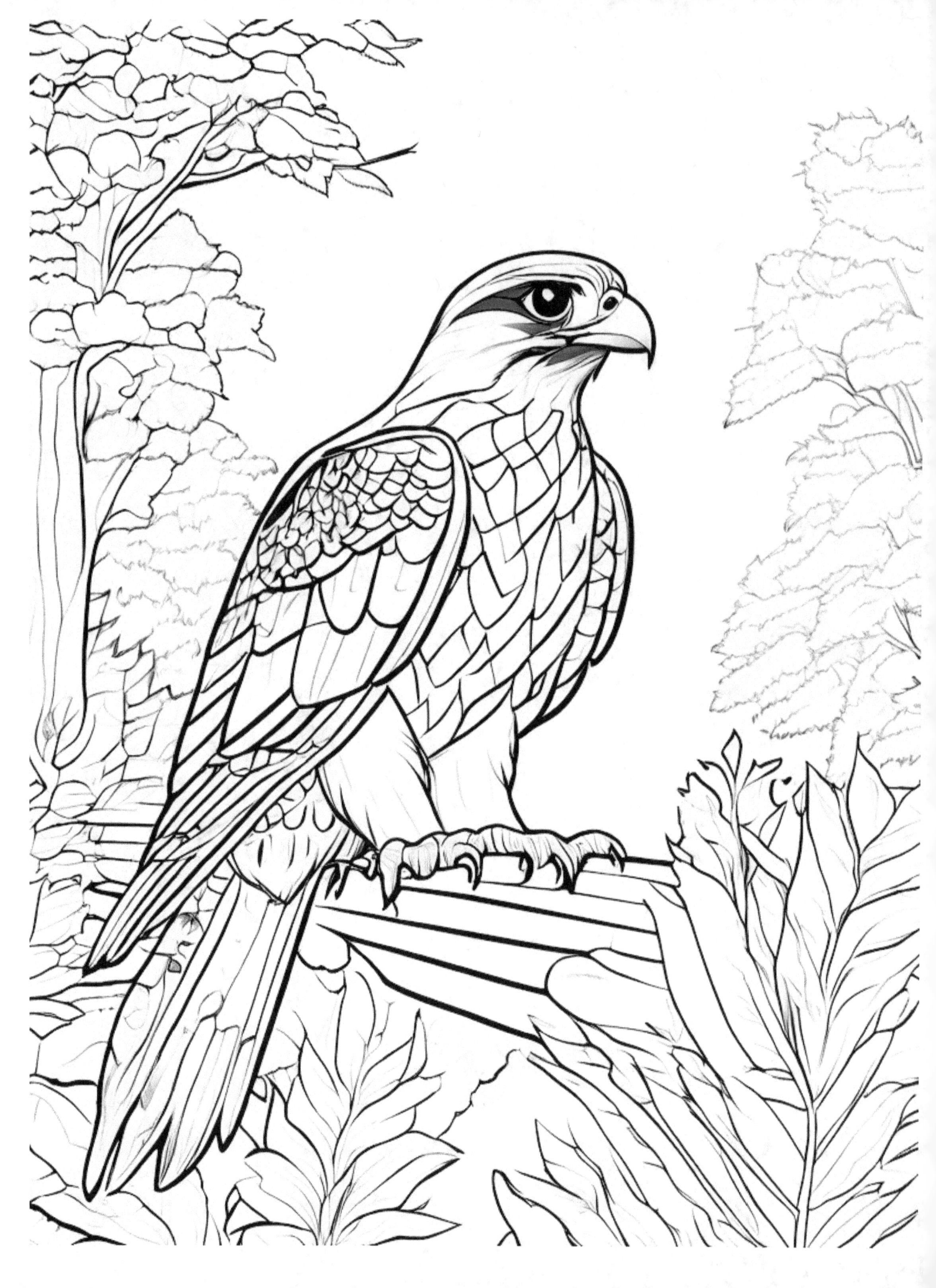

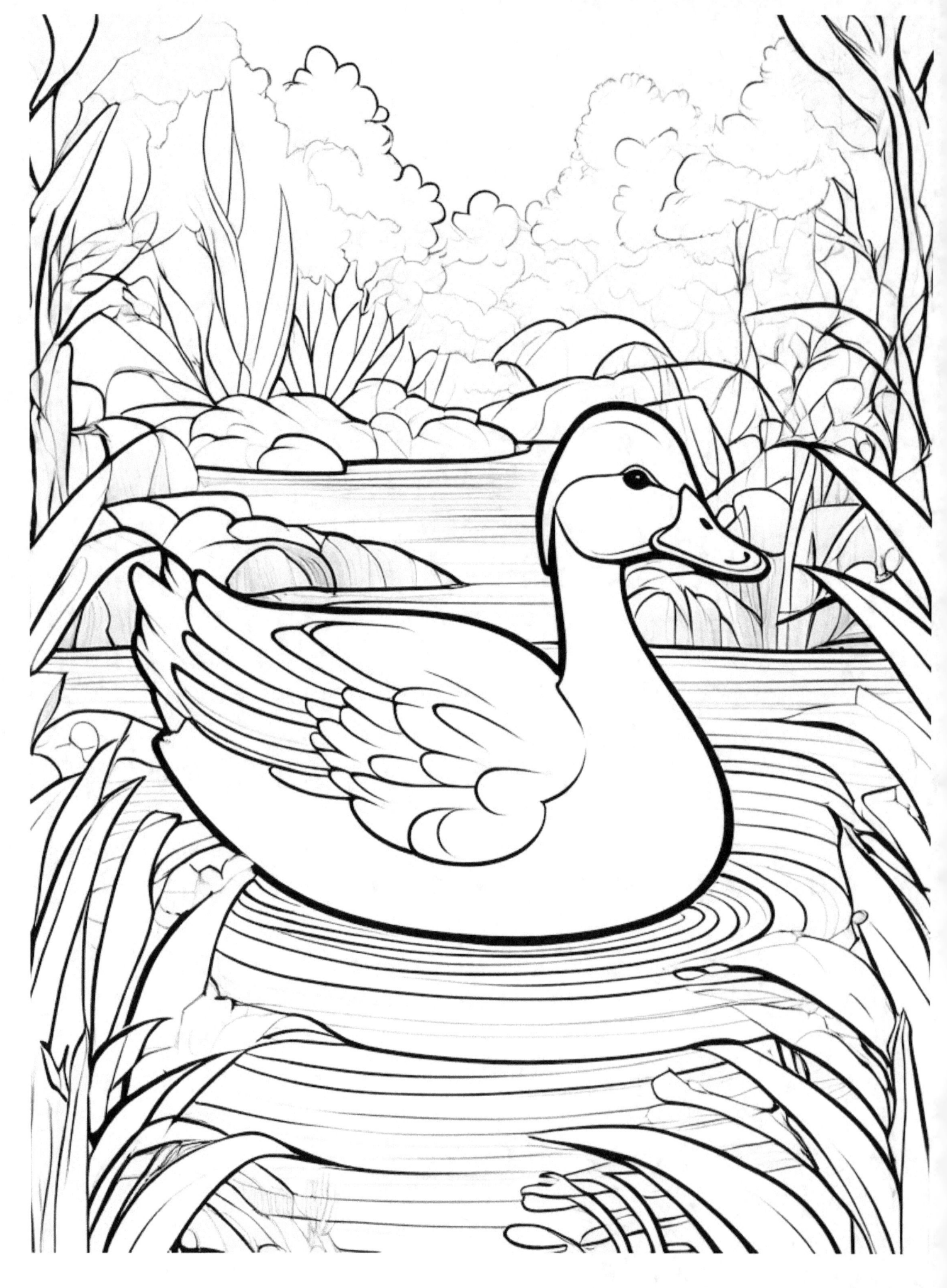

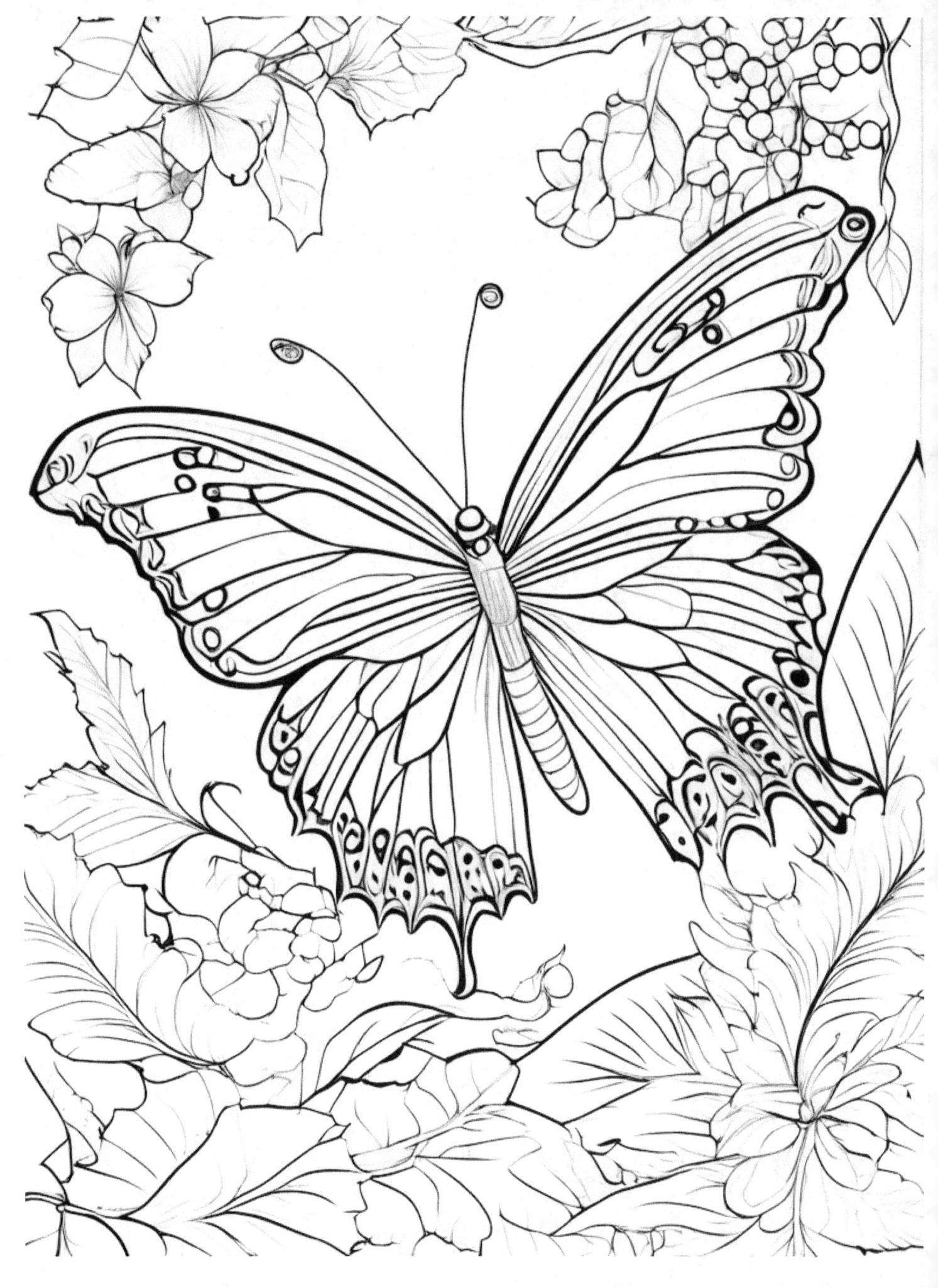

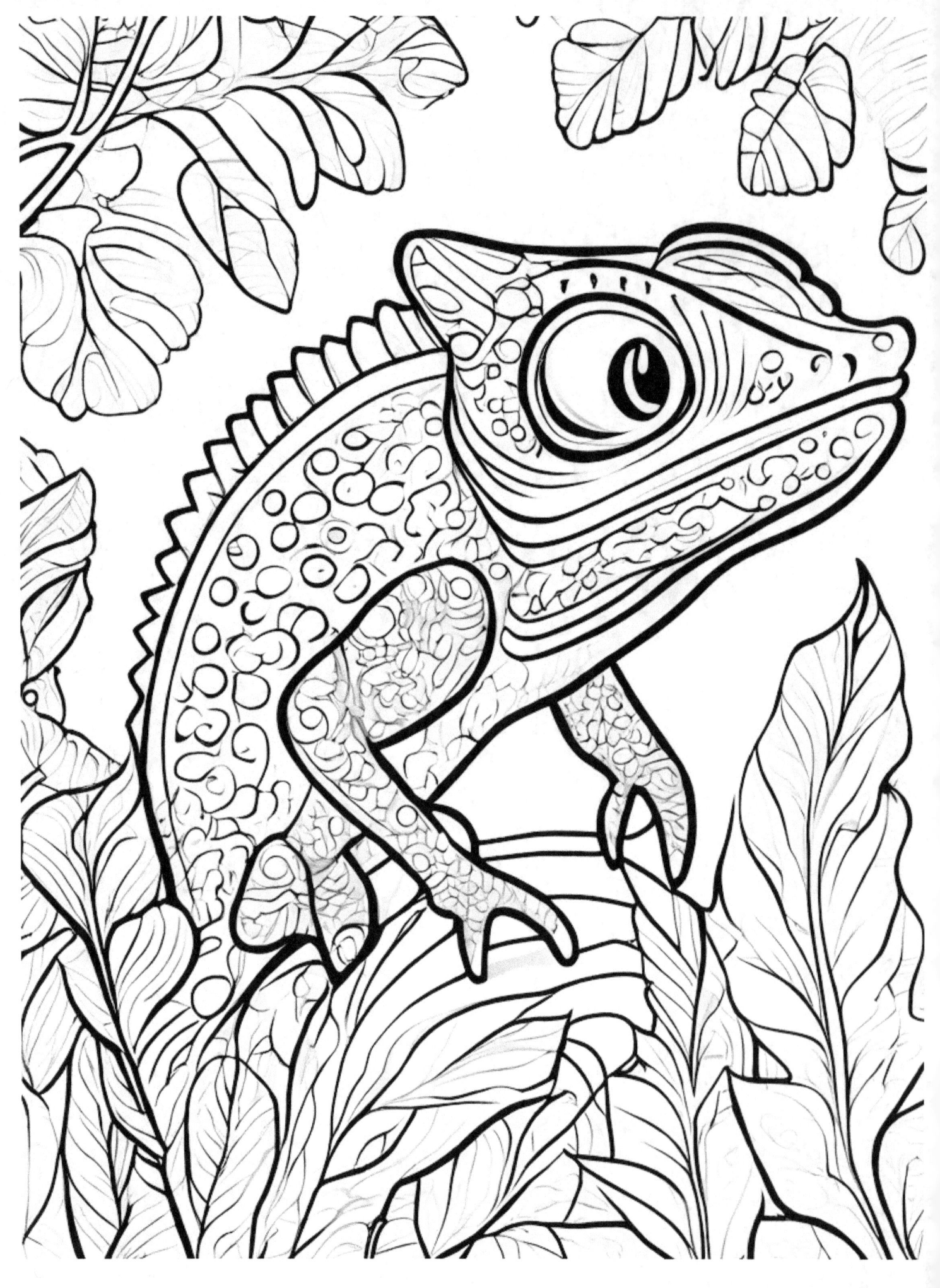

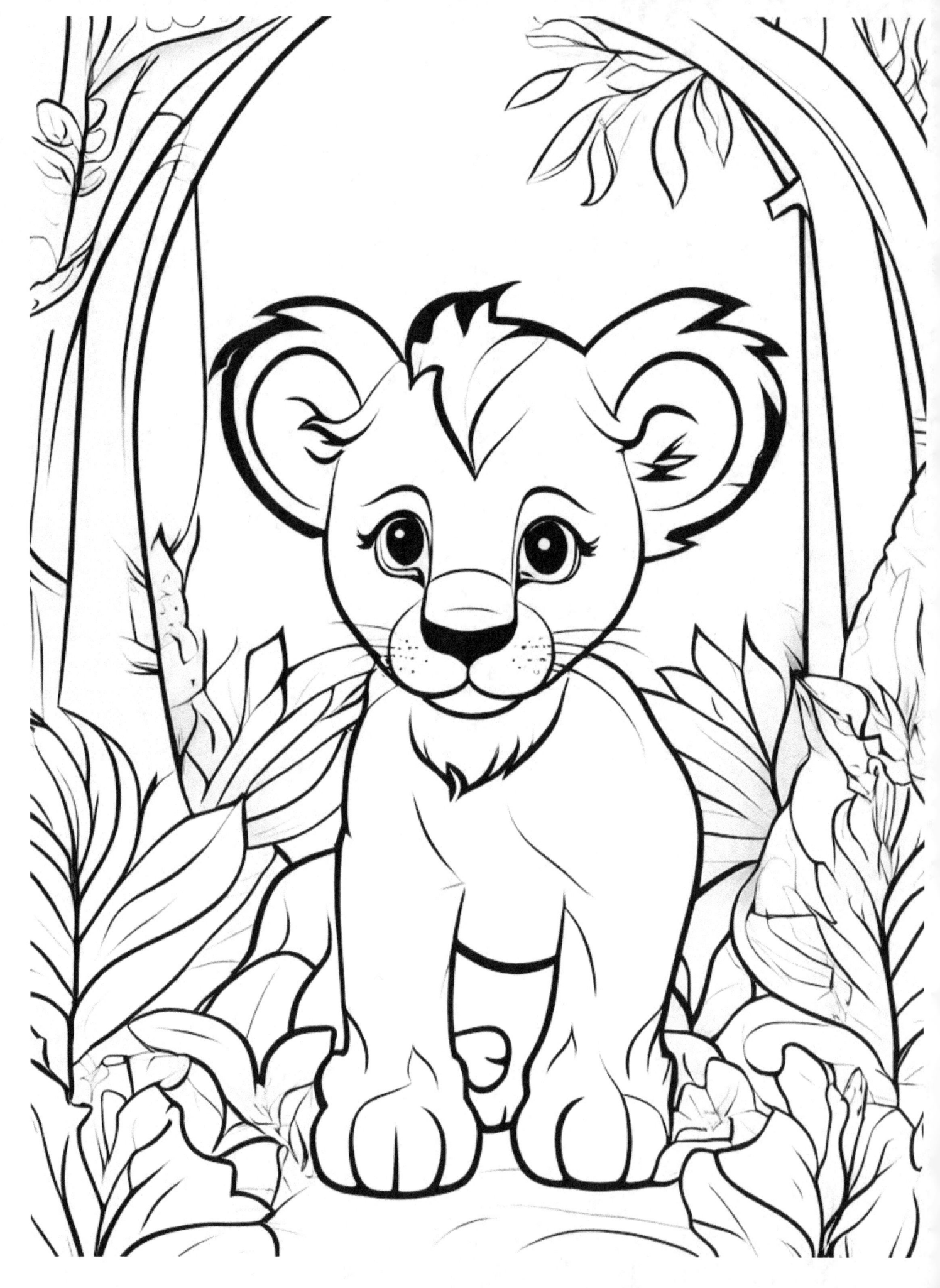

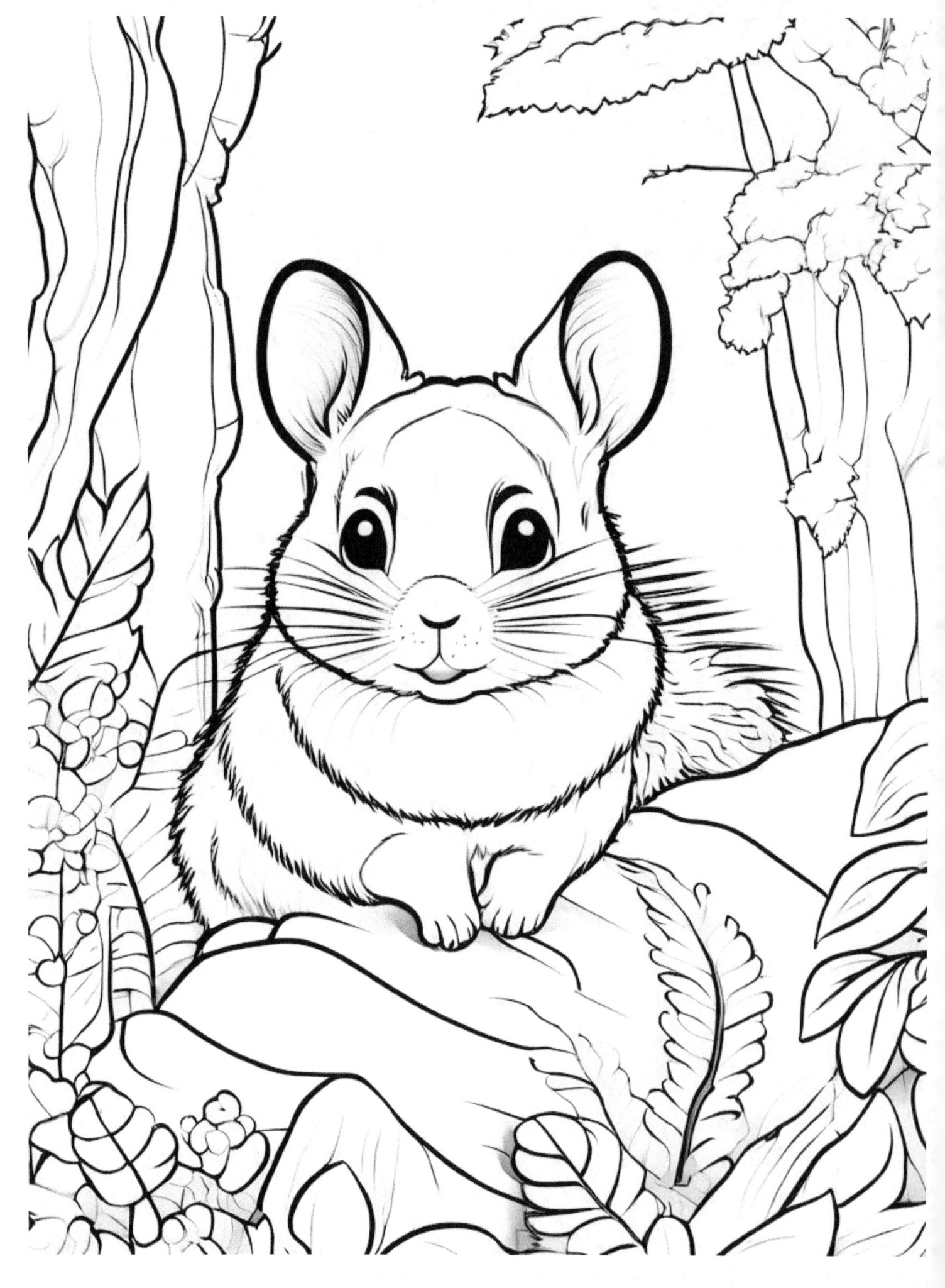

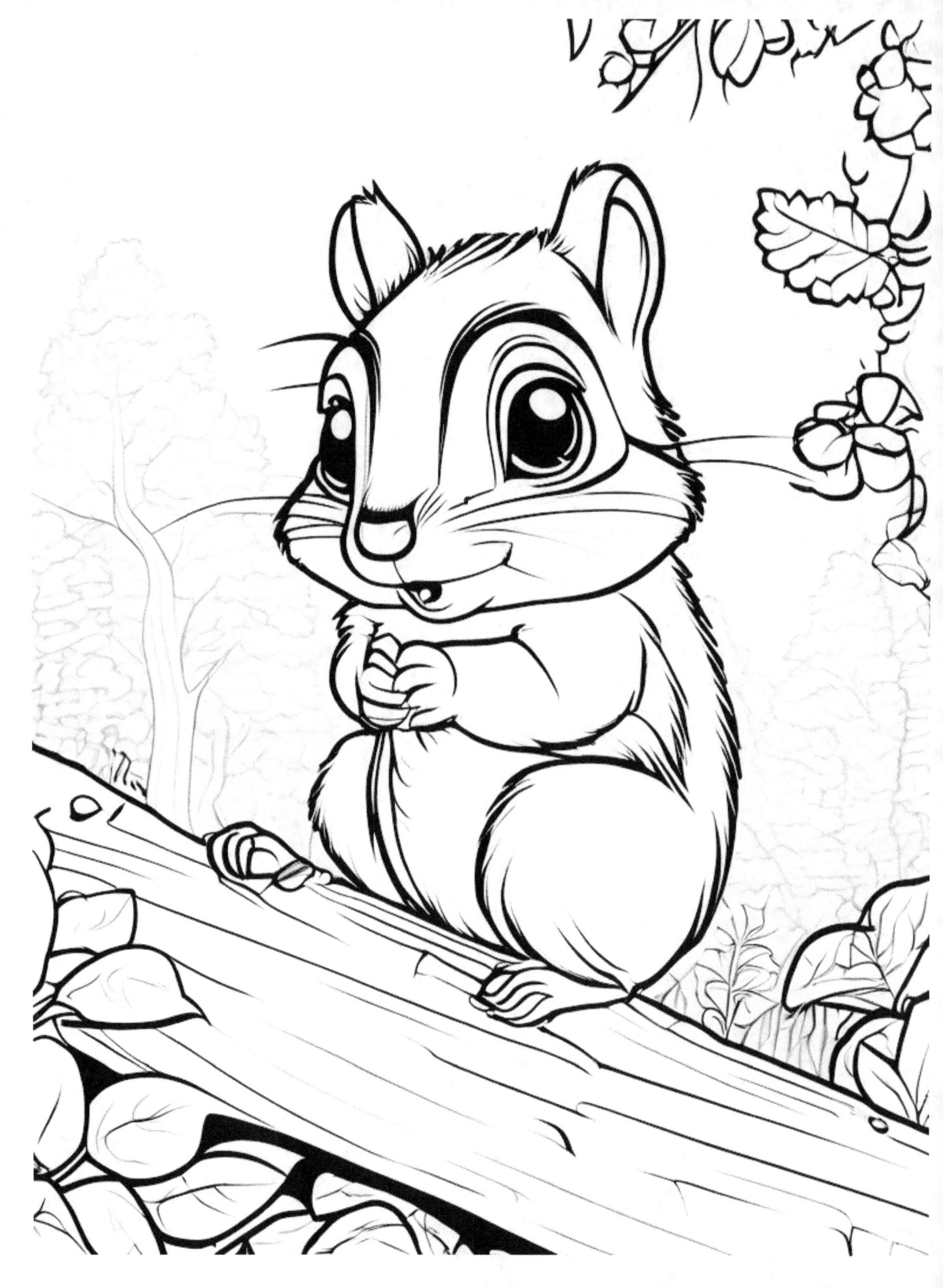

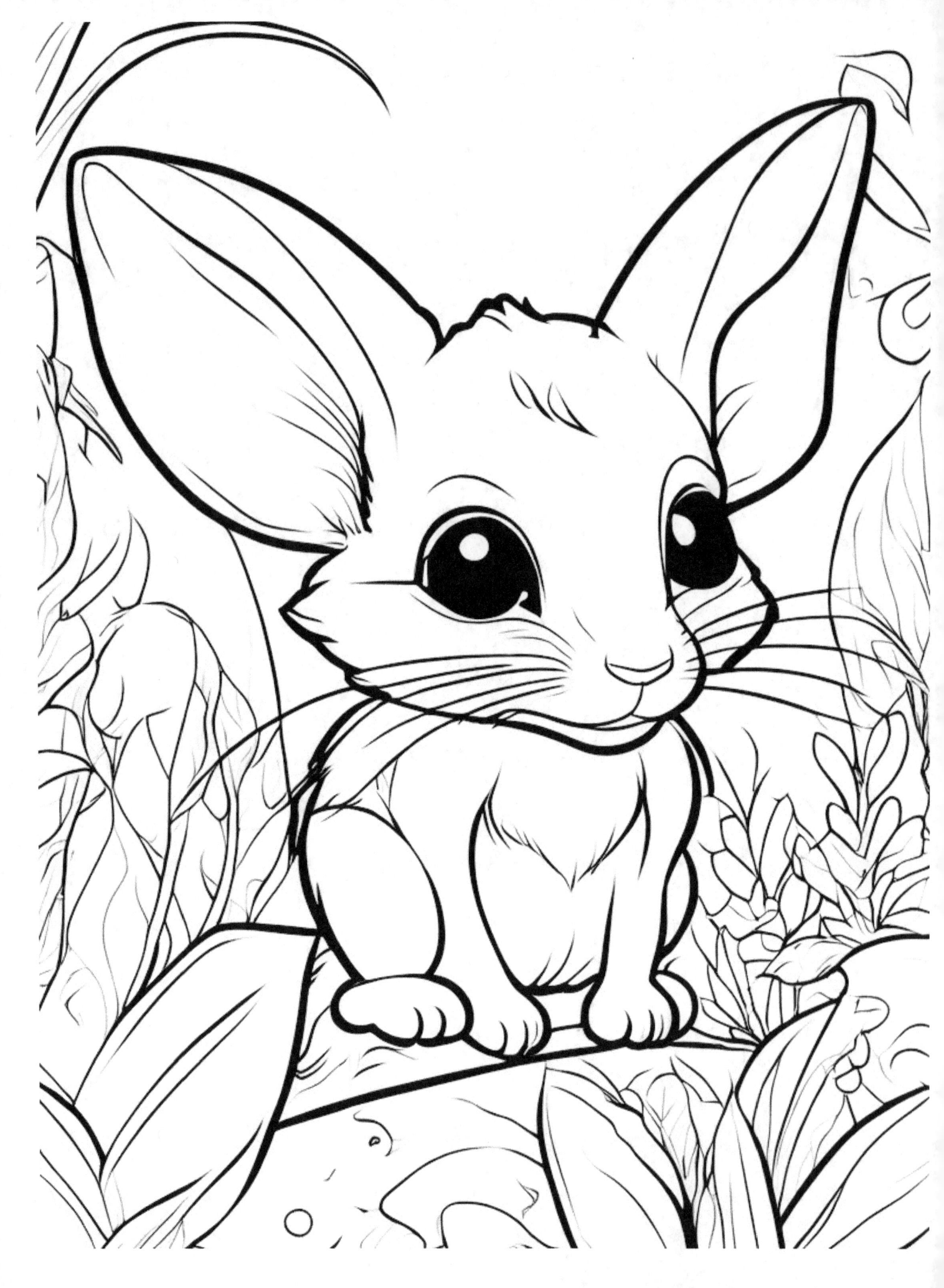

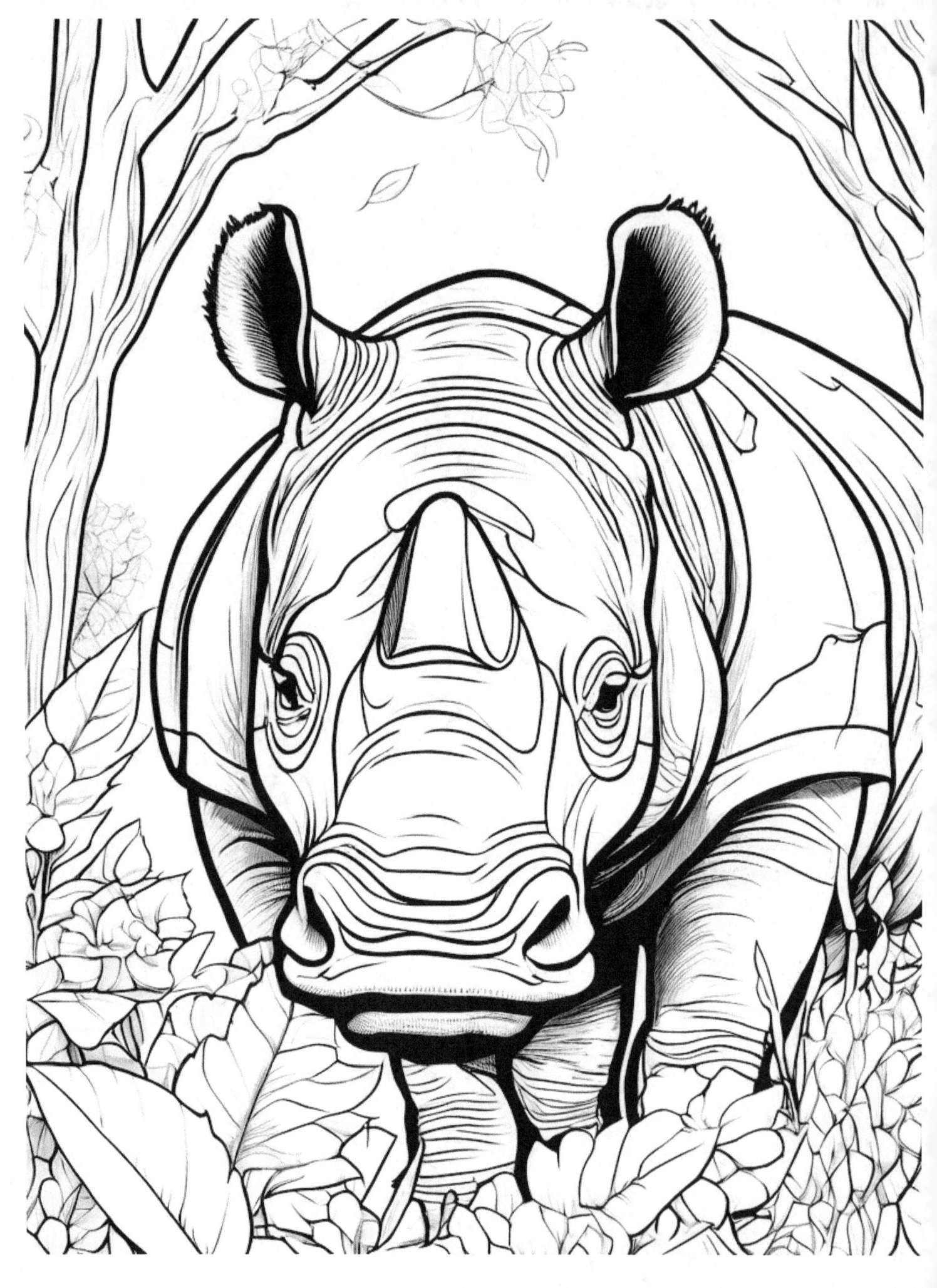

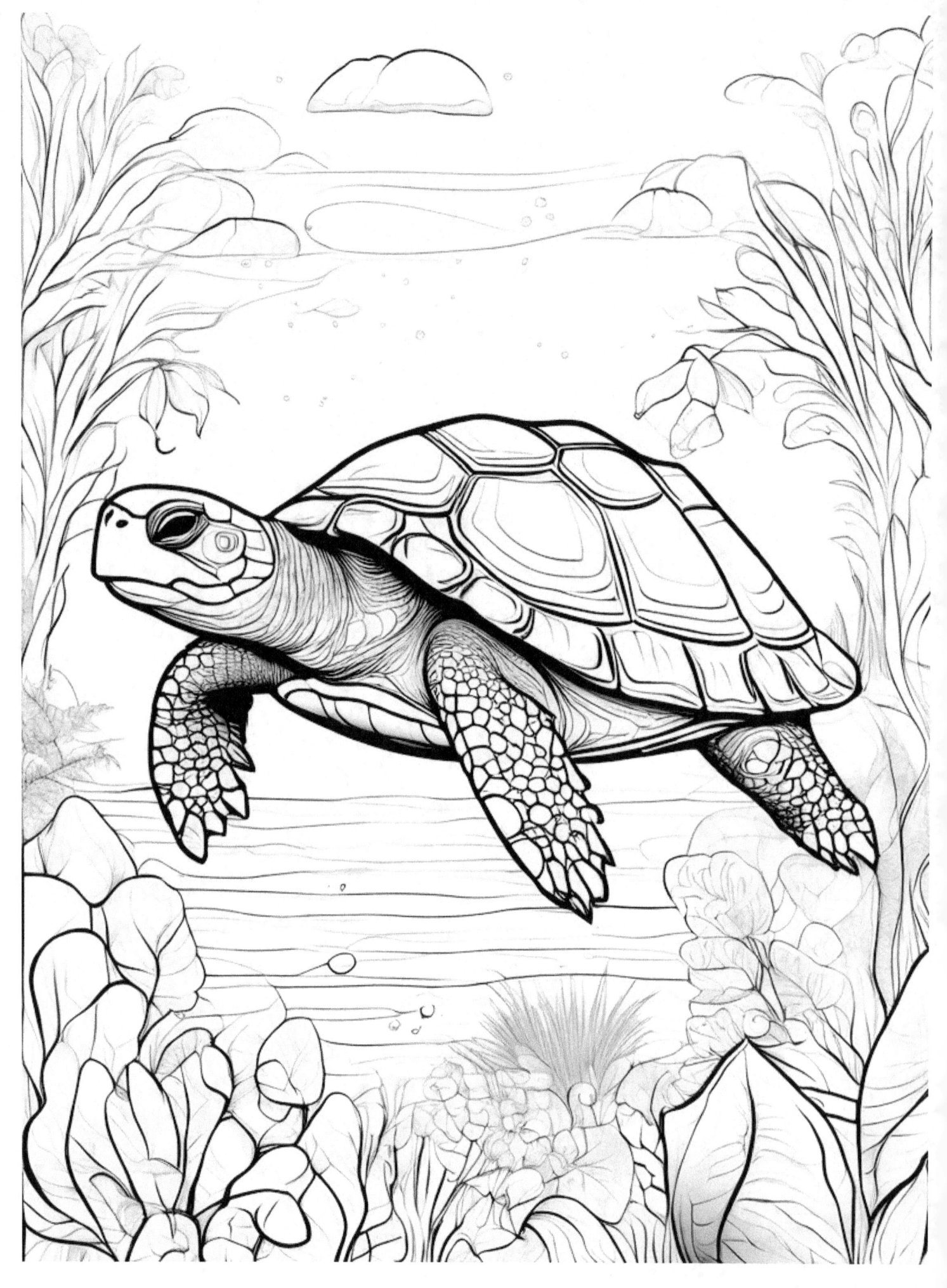

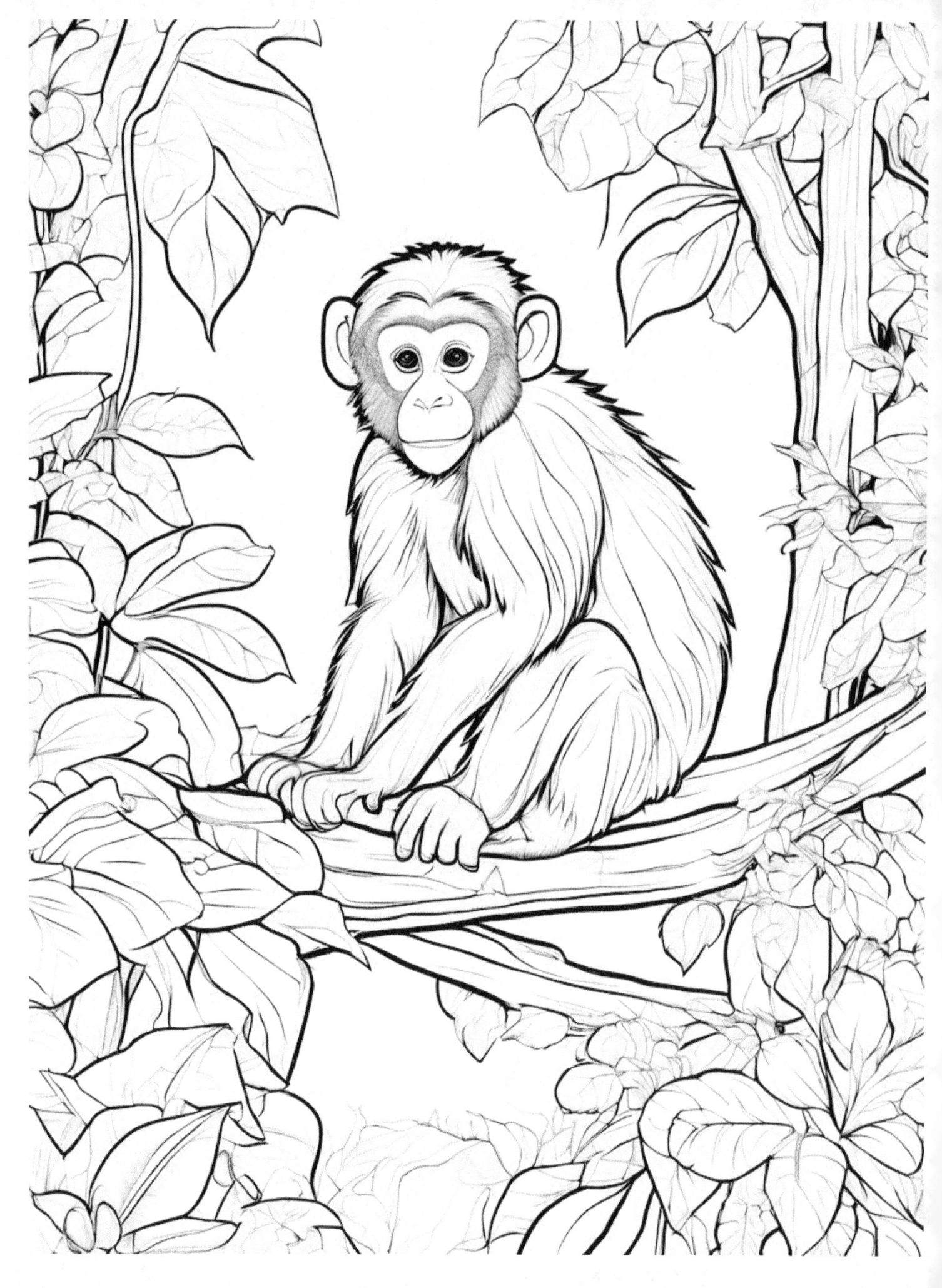

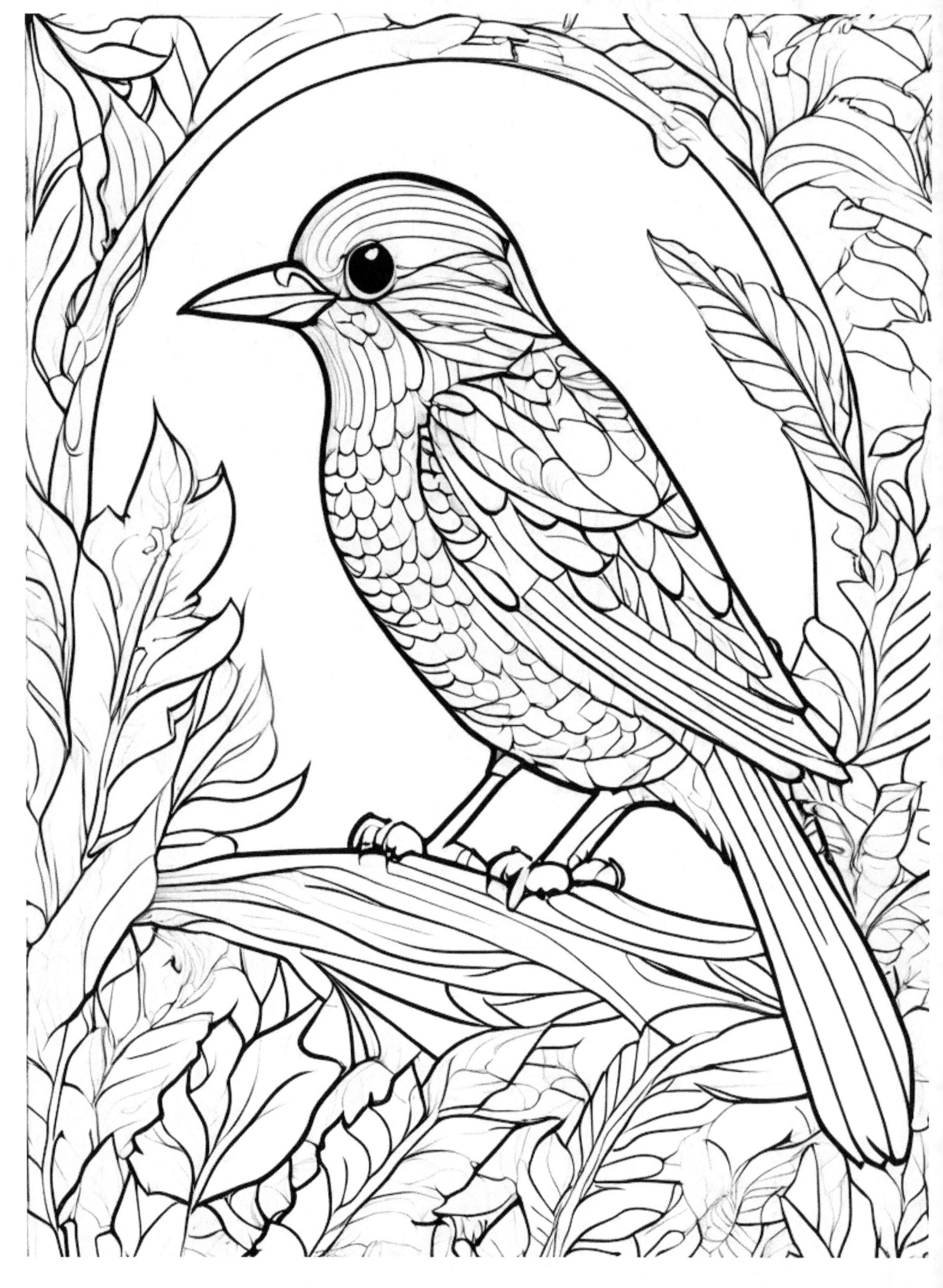

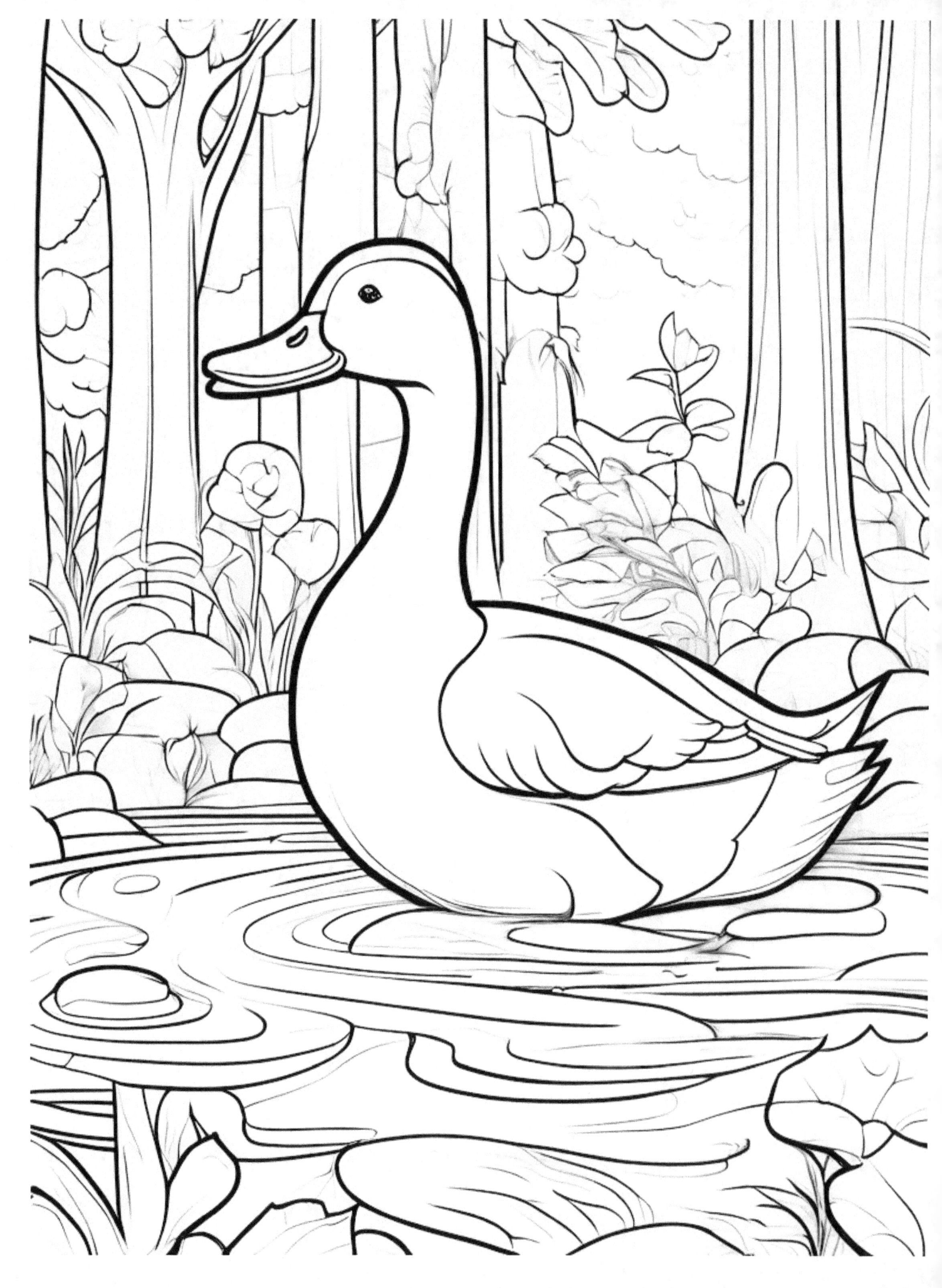

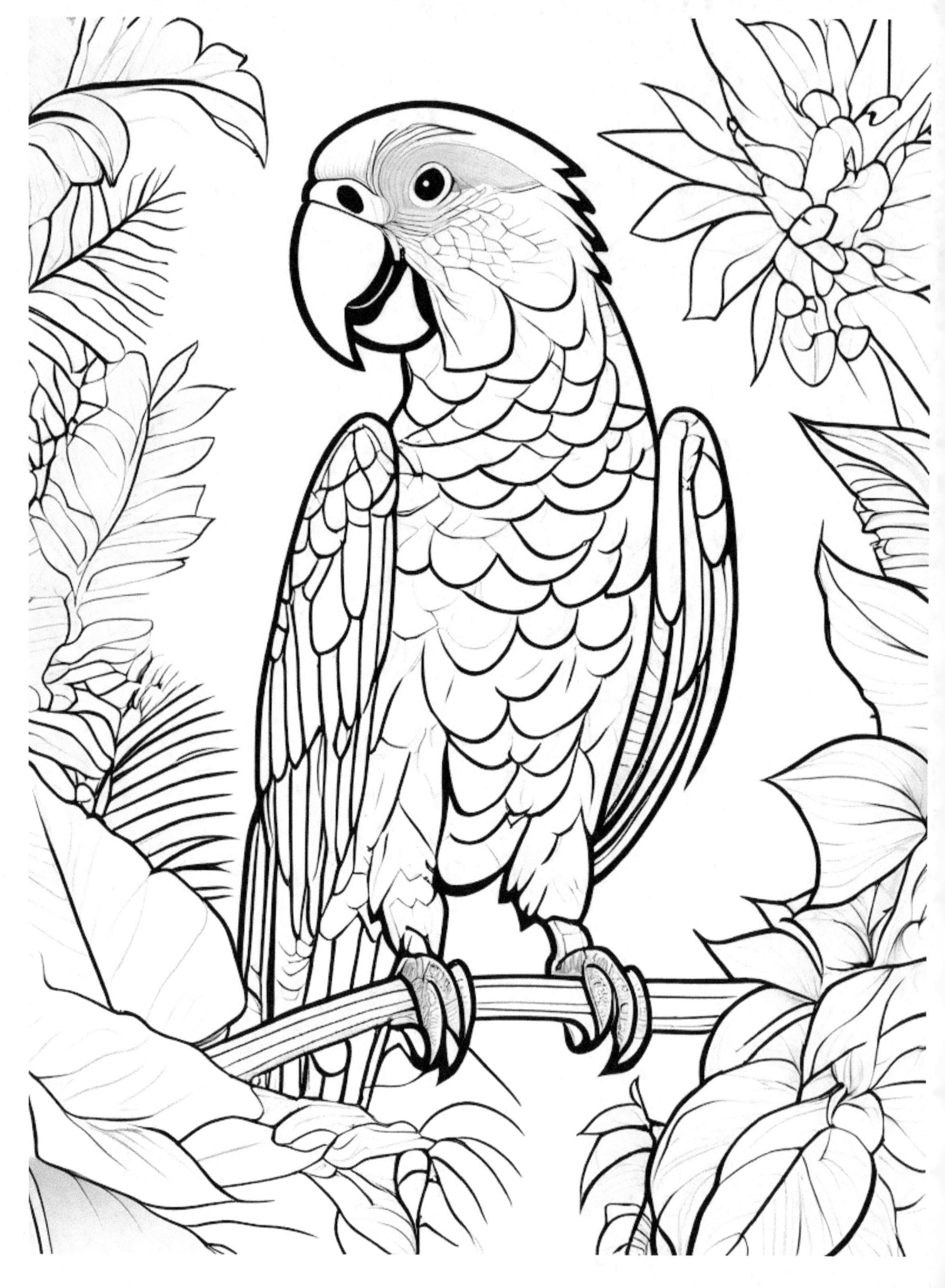

www.ingramcontent.com/pod-product-compliance
Lightning Source LLC
Chambersburg PA
CBHW082216220526
45470CB00010B/3197